BERLITZ®

✔ KT-382-742

MALTA

1991/1992 Edition

By the staff of Berlitz Guides

19th Printing
1991/1992 Edition

Updated or revised 1991, 1987, 1986, 1985, 1984, 1983, 1982,
1981

How to use our guide

- All the practical information, hints and tips that you will need before and during the trip start on page 102.

- For general background, see the sections Malta and the Maltese, p. 6, and A Brief History, p. 13.

- All the sights to see are listed between pages 26 and 83. Our own choice of sights most highly recommended is pinpointed by the Berlitz traveller symbol.

- Entertainment, nightlife and all other leisure activities are described between pages 84 to 93, while information on restaurants and cuisine is to be found on pages 94 to 101.

- Finally, there is an index at the back of the book, pp. 126–128.

Although we make every effort to ensure the accuracy of all the information in this book, changes occur incessantly. We cannot therefore take responsibility for facts, prices, addresses and circumstances in general that are constantly subject to alteration. Our guides are updated on a regular basis as we reprint, and we are always grateful to readers who let us know of any errors, changes or serious omissions they come across.

Text: Suzanne Patterson
Photography: Ken Welsh, p. 78 PRISMA/Schuster GmbH
Layout: Hanspeter Schmidt
We are grateful to Mr. and Mrs. Joseph Arrigo, Mr. and Mrs. Robert Hammond, Mr. and Mrs. James Pettigrew and Mr. J.G. Vassallo for their help in the preparation of this book. We would also like to thank the National Tourist Organization of Malta and Air Malta for their valuable assistance.
Cartography: Falk Falk-Verlag, Hamburg.

Contents

The Islands and the People		6
A Brief History		13
Where to Go		26
	Valletta	28
	Around Valletta	44
	Inland to Mdina and Rabat	50
	South-East Coast	56
	The North-West	58
	The Prehistoric Sites	63
	Gozo	70
	Victoria	72
	Towns and Villages	80
What to Do	Sports	84
	Shopping	88
	Festivals	90
	Nightlife	92
Dining out in Malta		94
Blueprint for a Perfect Trip (Practical Information)		102
Index		126

Maps		
	The Maltese Islands	9
	Malta	27
	Valletta Town Centre	31
	Valletta and Suburbs	45
	Mdina and Rabat	51
	Gozo and Comino	71
	Victoria (Rabat)	75

Cover picture: St. Julian's Bay

The Islands and the People

The strategic position of Malta, Gozo and Comino have made the islands of the Maltese archipelago a crossroads of history and often a bone of contention. But for the jet-age traveller, these Mediterranean islands, only 60 miles south of Sicily and 220 miles north of the deserts of Libya, are a good place for a beach holiday—with the added attraction of dozens of sights and monuments from a fascinating past.

Approached by air or sea, Malta seems arid and austere. But as you get nearer, the landscape of the main island softens with a special beauty. A pink-and-ochre rocky surface is filled with free-stone fences rambling over pockets of greenery, dotted with dozens of church belfries. In cobalt-blue harbours and tiny inlets, little multi-coloured *luzzu* fishing boats—with the fierce eyes of Osiris painted on their bows to ward off the evil eye—bob next to yachts, cruise-ships and mammoth oil tankers.

Inland, the countryside is full of contrasts. The scene is biblical—flat-topped houses against an arid background. Yet, at the time of the spring flowering,

the barren hills burst into colour. Horse-drawn carts vie for road space with big cars; 20th-century ideas mix strangely with religious traditions. On this pretty and paradoxical island, the traffic and bright red pillar boxes could be London's, and the pizzas seem Italian, but they couldn't be

6

more genuinely Maltese, as you'll soon find out.

Valletta, the capital city, is ringed by bastions. In the past they provided the islanders with protection. Today their architecture is admired by visitors from all over the world. For while there are still factories making small components

Malta in a nutshell: man and beast till the land beneath skyline of church towers and windmills.

or jeans or tinned tomato paste, one of Malta's biggest industries is tourism. New hotels line the bays and beaches north-west of Valletta; most of **7**

Malta in a Minute

Some of the information given below can be found in different sections of our guide, but for your convenience it is gathered together here for a quick briefing.

Geography   Malta, Gozo and Comino comprise the Republic of Malta, 60 miles south of Sicily in the Mediterranean Sea with an area of 122 square miles. Population 330,000. Travel time from London, about 3 hours Heathrow to Luqa.

Climate   Good months for visiting are April, May, June, October and November. July and August are hot. January is the coldest month.

Government   Became a democratic republic within the British Commonwealth on December 13, 1974.

Religion   Roman Catholic.

---

the year the islands bask in sunny holiday weather and in summer the temperature can soar. Wherever you are, the tempting dark-blue Mediterranean is never far away and always ready to refresh you.

The main island is just 95 square miles (one-sixth the size of greater London) and you can travel easily from place to place, by car, bus or taxi. Gozo is even smaller, only 26 square miles, and remains a rustic, unspoilt outpost. Between Malta and Gozo, tiny Comino has one square mile, one hotel and a handful of residents and tourists.

The population of the island nation is estimated to be about 340,000, of whom about one in ten live on Gozo. People have lived on the islands since Neolithic times, around 7,000 years ago. Colonized by almost every Mediterranean power— from the Phoenicians and Romans to the Knights of the Order of St. John and the British—the country became an independent nation in 1964.

From these different roots, the Maltese people have emerged. For the most part, they are sturdy, dark-haired and olive-skinned, almost all great swimmers and good sailors. Visitors are invariably impressed by the islanders who are among the most polite and good-natured in the world. They are proud and fun-loving and know how to laugh at themselves as well as with everybody else. Work gets

THE MALTESE ISLANDS

Labels on map: MEDITERRANEAN, SICILY, Marsalforn, Zebbug, Xaghra, Qala, Gharb, VICTORIA, Nadur, Mgarr, Comino, San Lawrenz, Kercem, Xewkija, Cominotto, Xlendi, Sannat, Gozo, Mellieha, Bugibba, St. Paul's Bay, Gharghur, St. Julian's, Sliema, VALLETTA, Zabbar, Naxxar, Birkirkara, Hamrun, Zejtun, Zebbieh, Mosta, Qormi, Paola, Tarxien, Marsaxlokk, Mgarr, Mdina, Luqa, Kirkop, Zebbug, Rabat, Siggiewi, Safi, Birzebbuga, Dingli, Zurrieq, Malta

0 2 4 6 8 10 km
0 2 4 6 miles
N

done—but it's never taken too seriously.

Everyone speaks Malti, a language related to Arabic, with some Italian and a little French thrown in. It's an exotic tongue for foreigners. The Malti for "street", for example, is *triq*. With many consonants, the pronunciation is difficult. *Xewkija* on Gozo is pronounced "shoo-KEE-yah". But tourists have few language problems, as English is taught in the schools. Almost all Maltese speak it fairly well.

The addition of the English language and certain Anglo-Saxon customs and food to Mediterranean ways has given rise to a unique local style. Read the hand-painted signs of Malta for a vocabulary lesson: "The Up-to-Date Garage", "The Still-Alive Bar", "The In-tact Boutique", "The Perfection Confectionery".

Malta became Christian after St. Paul was shipwrecked there in A.D. 60. Today, in Rabat, you can visit the spot where the apostle is said to have stayed. Religion is taken seriously and there are wayside chapels everywhere. Each town and parish is fiercely proud of its church. Keeping up with the Joneses in Malta means keeping up with the neighbouring town's church and building a bigger, better one next time round.

The explosions you hear on weekends all summer long come from religious festivities or *festi*. These are well-attended events with parades, bands and fireworks. The churches take out their best silver objects and damask trappings; the **9** streets are decorated with huge statues of saints and are thronged with people. You'll hear Holy Masses, but sense a festive atmosphere as well.

Malta has produced several good local artists, though some of the finest paintings found in the islands were done by the Italians Caravaggio and Mattia Preti. More contemporary are the sculptures of Antonio Sciortino. Many of his figures, full of grace and movement, can be seen on display. Local artisans' work, hand-blown glass, silver filigree, weaving, lace and pottery are undergoing an enthusiastic revival.

The islands are full of fascination and fun. The mystery becomes palpable as you wander through the prehistoric ruins of Ħaġar Qim or visit Gozo's Ġgantija, with the wind whistling eerily around you. No one can fully explain the strange lost civilizations that built them there.

But nobody will be needed to help you enjoy the pleasures of the warm sandy beaches, the rock bathing and myriad water sports. A surprise lies around every corner: children playing with a pet goat; an ancient bare-footed crone clicking her bobbins to produce spiderwebs of lace; a *karrozzin* (surrey with

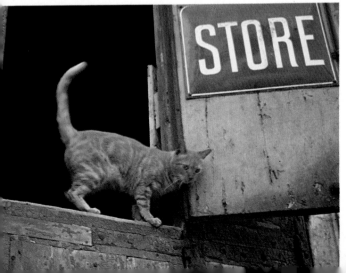

a fringe on top); or a *dghajsa* (a colourful water-taxi) plying its trade.

Whatever your interests—whether archaeological, artistic, religious or sporting—you'll find something to satisfy you in Malta. And nobody will criticize if you just want to soak up the sun at a swimming pool with the prospect of a leisurely lunch by the sea later on.

Mediterranean waves wash the golden sands of Gozo's Ramla beach, big enough for holiday throngs; ginger cat, left, surveys Valletta.

A Brief History

Often ruled, never truly dominated, the Maltese islands command a striking place in European history. Their past is marked by violence, intrigue and courage shown during battles fought over the centuries for the strategically situated islands. Eyed covetously, ruled by many different factions and nations, Malta has been called "a palimpsest of history" —meaning an original manuscript erased and re-written over many times.

But long before recorded history, a civilization of a kind had dawned on Malta. In the Stone, Copper and Bronze ages, the island boasted an organized society, capable of producing quite complex architectural structures.

The first settlers—probably peasant-farmers—had crossed over from Sicily around 5000 B.C. (for a comment on prehistoric dates, see p. 63). Fascinating traces of these early inhabitants and the generations that followed them can still be seen all over the islands. Their driving force was a primitive religious cult probably related to death and fertility.

Profile of fishing boats and colour of stone are distinctively Maltese.

You can visit many of the prehistoric sites. One extraordinary underground complex of cave-like tombs on Malta is at Paola. Called the Hypogeum, it was in use from about 3200–2500 B.C. Its elliptical-shaped rooms and passages served as a burial chamber and perhaps temple. The basic architectural forms found here also appear above ground in such enormous stone temples as Ġgantija on Gozo or Ħaġar Qim on Malta.

Some of the best of these prehistoric buildings were built during the Tarxien era (about 3200–2500 B.C.), named after the place where several of them were found. They were a stunning feat of construction for such supposedly unsophisticated people. But then the whole temple-building civilization disappeared, possibly as a result of invasion, although other theories include a plague or the pressures of overpopulation.

The next wave of immigrants appears to have come from southern Italy. This group, who used the Tarxien temples as a burial ground, were known as "the Cemetery People". They were followed by others, who built a defensive wall at Borġ in-Nadur, and settled in fortified villages. **13**

The Great "Cart Track" Mystery

Parts of the stony land of Malta and Gozo are criss-crossed with prehistoric "cart tracks". They are not always of the same width, and were probably not even made by carts.

The tracks have been found all over village sites and seem to have been used for some kind of vehicle. The ancient buggies were probably "slide carts", with two shafts attached to a draught animal which dragged two stones attached by a crossbar behind it. On the bar might have been placed building materials, agricultural produce, or other loads.

Carthaginians and Romans

Recorded Maltese history began around the 9th century B.C., with the arrival of the Phoenicians. Later, in the 6th century B.C., came traders from the Phoenician colony of Carthage. A brilliant Mediterranean people, their colonization was to last for centuries.

Another strong influence in Maltese history was that of the Greeks. Although they never colonized the nation, the presence of many coins and inscriptions suggests that they visited Malta between the 6th and 7th centuries B.C.

Malta's strategic significance came back into the spotlight during the Punic Wars (the three wars in the 3rd and 2nd centuries B.C. between Phoenician Carthage and Rome). The island was fought over by the great powers but it finally fell to the Roman consul Tiberius Sempronius in 218 B.C.

The Carthaginians had built their central capital on a hilltop, where Mdina is now, and the Romans took this over as their base, fortifying it and building luxurious villas in and around it. You can still see a good reconstruction of one of these typical Roman houses, between Mdina and Rabat.

One of Malta's most important historical events happened during Roman rule. In A.D. 60, St. Paul and St. Luke were shipwrecked on Malta, somewhere around the area now known as St. Paul's Bay. Paul's preaching in Jerusalem and Caesarea had caused such an outcry among the religious leaders that the Romans had arrested him, partly for his own safety. During the subsequent enquiry, Paul, a Roman citizen, appealed to Caesar for justice and it was when he and Luke were travelling as prisoners from Caesarea to Rome that the ship foundered on the rocks of Malta.

Street corner shrine amidst typical Valletta balconies: delicately sculpted stone statue of St. Peter of Alcántara.

For a whole winter they stayed in a cave at Mdina-Rabat, and St. Paul preached the Gospel. His message and the miracles that happened in his presence were sufficient to convert the Roman Governor, Publius, who subsequently became the first Bishop of Malta and was later martyred and canonized. Despite different governments and the spreading of Islam by the Arabs, Malta has remained fundamentally Christian from St. Paul's day to this.

The Dark Ages and Arab Rule

As the Roman Empire declined, Malta's history becomes obscure. In 870 the Arabs became the new rulers. Although they tolerated Christianity, many islanders seem to have emigrated or to have become Moslem. At that time, slavery was a big business, and trading was carried on by both Maltese and Arabs. The victims were mainly Christians from neighbouring countries.

Two centuries of Arab rule left an indelible impression on **15**

the island, particularly on the
language. The Arabs also introduced the cultivation of cotton
and citrus fruit, which became
very important to the economy.
Malta was now a prosperous
Mediterranean trading nation.

But quarrelling factions
among the rulers soon made
the island ripe for conquest—
this time by Count Roger
the Norman, son of Tancred
de Hauteville, in 1090–91.
Roger, who had inherited a
principality in southern Italy
from his father, wanted to
ensure the defence of Sicily by
controlling Malta. His conquest
16 of St. Paul's Bay and, later,

Mdina was relatively easy and
Malta became part of the
Kingdom of Sicily. The new
ruler was fairly liberal and let
the islanders govern themselves
by local councils. Moslems
were tolerated, and the Christian church was encouraged to
renew and expand itself.

During the Crusades, Malta
was a key link in Christianity's
line of defence against the
Moslems, even though Maltese
Moslems were still living there.

After being attached to Sicily, Malta passed into the hands
of the Swabians and then to
the French king's (Louis IX's)
brother, Charles of Anjou.
The French remained in
power until being ousted by
Peter I of Aragon in 1282,
when the islands became an
Aragonese possession.

Under the uneasy joint
Spanish-Sicilian rule, Malta
was exploited by overseas
noblemen only interested in
the country as a source of revenue. The Maltese themselves
worked at trading, slaving and
piracy to provide taxes and in-
come for the owners.

By the 15th century, local
self-government had reached a
certain level of maturity with
an administrative body known
as the Università governing
and distributing food supplies.
Tired of exploitation by for-

eign nobility, the Università managed to raise a substantial sum of money to bring Malta into a more secure relationship with Spain. Thus, in 1428, the Spanish King Alfonso V declared Malta "reunited in perpetuity" to the Crown, which administered the island directly, without the landlords.

Meanwhile, the islands were continually and repeatedly raided by Berbers, Turks and Saracens. By the 16th century, the morale of the country was sinking and the economy was on the decline.

The Knights' Arrival

But other developments in the Mediterranean area were already taking place that would change Maltese fortunes. In the early 16th century, Sultan Suleiman the Magnificent and the Turks more or less ruled the seas in the name of Islam. They had long harassed the Knights of the Order of St. John on Rhodes, and finally occupied that island on New Year's Day, 1523, after a six-month siege. This left the knights homeless.

The courageous Grand Master, Philippe Villiers de l'Isle-Adam, led his soldiers to Sicily and Italy. But Europe's loyalties were divided between Francis I of France and Charles V, Holy Roman Emperor and King of Spain and Sicily. Finding a permanent settlement for the knights was a thorny problem.

After seven years of negotiations, the knights reluctantly agreed to take over Malta and the island was granted to the Order nearly rent-free—in exchange for the token payment of one falcon a year (the famous "Maltese falcon", though not much to do with the film of that name). So, in 1530, the Grand Master with his 4,000 men moved into Malta.

Though the islanders were uneasy about the new occupants at first, their rights and privileges were respected. The knights built fortifications and living quarters in Birgu (later called Vittoriosa) and generally strengthened the area that is now known as Valletta (the Sceberras peninsula between Grand and Marsamxett harbours). The capital became the new focus of interest on Malta and attention was taken away from the old town of Mdina.

The Grand Master Villiers de l'Isle-Adam died in 1534, was succeeded by several others and finally by Jean Parisot de la Valette in 1557. His name was to become famous in the island's history.

The Knights of St. John

The full title of the Order was the Knights Hospitalers of St. John of Jerusalem. The Order was founded in Jerusalem in the 11th century when some Italian merchants obtained permission from the Moslem caliph to set up a hospice for Christian pilgrims. The calling of the brothers was principally to care for the sick, but in time the emphasis shifted from the medical and religious arms of the Order to the knights' military task: that of fighting the infidel.

In 1187 the knights were driven from Jerusalem by Saladin and had to move on to Acre and then Cyprus, retreating finally to the island of Rhodes in 1308. Though the Turks laid siege to the island several times, it wasn't until 1522, when they were attacked by Suleiman (the Magnificent), that the knights were forced to surrender.

The knights took vows of poverty, chastity and obedience and were divided into three main grades: Knights of Justice (bona fide aristocrats from all over Europe, who wore the 8-pointed cross, now called the Maltese cross), Sergeants at Arms (who acted as both soldiers and nurses), and Chaplains (who worked in the hospitals and churches).

The knights were grouped under eight *langues* or "tongues", three of them French, as France was divided in the 13th century into France, Provence and Auvergne. The other *langues* were Aragon, Castille, Italy, Germany and England. After the Reformation in the 16th century the English *langue* had ceased to exist. A joint *langue* of England and Bavaria was set up in 1784. Each *langue* was headed by a *pilier*, who had a set function; thus the *pilier* of Italy was Grand Admiral; the *pilier* of Provence was financial and ordnance manager; the *pilier* of France was head of the Order's hospitals, etc.

In the 16th century, the knights had over 650 *commanderies* in Europe, and huge estates all over the continent. Their supreme head was the Grand Master, elected for life, and subject only to the Pope.

As the years progressed the knights lapsed into careless and dissolute ways. Discipline became lax, corruption crept in and internal dissensions added to the failing powers of the Order. A fitting tribute to the original motives of the Hospitalers is the St. John Ambulance Association; the Order of St. John is still a sovereign Order with headquarters in Rome.

Philippe Villiers de l'Isle-Adam led knights to Malta in 1530.

For years, Turks had been attacking the knights on Malta, determined to take possession of the tiny island for its strategic position astride the Mediterranean sea routes. Another menace to the peace was a North-African pirate called Dragut. He had his own designs on Gozo, devastating it in 1546 and taking over 6,000 Gozitans away as slaves in 1551. Dragut then joined the Turks, adding his own forces to the growing threat to Christendom all over the Mediterranean.

The Great Siege

Suleiman the Magnificent decided the time was ripe for Islam to strike in a big way and began an unprecedented build-up of troops. This was reported to Grand Master de la Valette, who frantically sent out an ap- **19**

The Great Siege: fresco depicts brave standoff of forces in 1565.

peal for assistance to friendly quarters, but no help came, and on May 19, 1565, a Turkish fleet of 138 galleys disembarked 38,000 troops at Marsaxlokk Bay.

This looked like a disaster for de la Valette and his 600 knights, with only 9,000 troops and eight galleys at his disposal. The Turks—under Admiral Piali and Mustapha Pasha—felt sure they would win. Among their troops was a special corps of 4,000 janissaries—a group trained for fighting and killing only.

The knights carried out one of the most valiant defences in all history, though things went badly throughout. Fort St. Elmo was finally overrun in a battle fought to the last man. After the massacre, the Turks tied the knights' corpses to crosses and set them afloat in the Grand Harbour, to the horror of the others opposite at Birgu. Dragut the pirate was also killed in this battle, struck by a cannonball. He was to be sorely missed by the Islamic forces. The place where he fell is called Dragut point, on Marsamxett Harbour, opposite Fort St. Elmo.

De la Valette reinforced his defences at Birgu and Senglea. The critical moment of the siege had come, and Queen Elizabeth of England instructed prayers to be said in all the churches of her realm. All Christendom worried, but nobody came to help. Throughout the terrible summer of 1565, as heat, disease and dwindling food supplies plagued them, the two sides battled on in their holy war. The whole Maltese population fought along with the knights, fiercely resisting the invaders.

Despite all their troops, their explosives and their dedication, the Turks were gradually worn down. The fact that there was often disagreement between their two top commanders didn't help matters. In one assault alone, the Turks lost 2,500 men.

But the knights, too, had their problems, losing both irreplaceable men and strategic positions to the Turks. Even de la Valette (though he was 72) threw himself violently into battle. His courageous action came at a low moment for the knights and was a great encouragement to his men.

Outside help for the Maltese and knights finally arrived with the Sicilian Viceroy, Garcia de Toledo, who brought reinforcements he had mustered with difficulty after renewed pleas from de la Valette.

By late summer, the Turks had run out of supplies, firm leadership and spirit and on September 8th, 1565, the siege was lifted and what was left of the attack force sailed away; most historians reckon well over two-thirds of their forces were lost. There was general rejoicing in Malta, though the main island had been devastated.

With money from the knights and European powers, plans were quickly drawn up for a new city between the two long harbours, in the area known as Sceberras. The knights obtained the help of Laparelli, the Pope's own architect. The cost was astronomical, but the kings of Europe sent generous gifts to support the project. Named after the courageous de la Valette, Valletta was born.

During the two final centuries of the knights' rule, Malta grew and prospered. Trading activities were renewed and developed, and there was a surge of grandiose building projects. After Laparelli, Gerolamo Cassar—a Maltese architect—took over, and is responsible for much of the way Valletta looks today: a harmonious early Baroque style tempered by a classic approach.

At about this time Mediterranean traders were beginning to feel the effects of the discovery of the alternative route (round the Cape of Good Hope) to the riches of India; and by the 18th century, with the emphasis of the main trading activities turned towards America, the prosperity of former years waned. The Order, too, was declining into a somewhat dissolute middle age. With the French Revolution of 1789, and the downfall of the aristocracy and church of France, the knights suffered another blow, losing a great deal of prestige—and revenue (a huge proportion had been French).

Enter Napoleon

In 1798, while planning his Empire-building projects, Napoleon came to the same conclusion other military minds had reached over the centuries. Realizing that Malta would be a valuable strategic outpost, he sailed into Marsaxlokk harbour on June 10, 1798, and went to Valletta, where he presented the knights with an ultimatum to pack up and leave. Where others had failed, Napoleon succeeded. The Grand Master, de Hompesch, meekly gave in, and after centuries of residence the world's most famous military Order duly departed.

Napoleon started energetically promulgating new laws, but then he also left, only six days after the knights. The subsequent two-year reign of the French was nasty and unpleasant. They came as conquerors and looters and were highly unpopular with the people and the Church. This encouraged the Maltese to embark on an insurrection that lasted on and off for 18 months. With troops sent by the King of Naples joining in on the Maltese side, and that scourge of the French, Admiral Nelson, patrolling the Mediterranean, Napoleon's soldiers were forced to capitulate in 1800. In 1802, the Treaty of Amiens formally restored Malta to the Order of St. John.

Great Britain, now approaching the height of her sea-power, had meanwhile become aware of Malta's value as a naval base. After informally occupying the islands and administering them through Alexander Ball, Britain finally had her possession of the territory formally recognized by the Treaty of Paris in 1814, and again during the Congress of Vienna in the following year. Thus, Malta entered a period of British rule that was to last until 1964. Even then, British forces were to stay on, using bases in the islands, until 1979.

British Rule
During the next century, the population of the islands grew considerably, while the economy fluctuated. Agricultural changes introduced by the British included potato farming (which flourished) and the silk industry (which soon died). Cotton production, once all-important, declined. New water sources were found and vineyards expanded.

In 1813, when a plague epidemic killed a fifth of the population, Sir Thomas Maitland became governor. Sir Thomas brought autocratic rule to Malta, and was nicknamed "King Tom". He dismissed the traditional local, self-governing body of the Università, and made sweeping reforms to bring Malta into line with the British judiciary system—though old practices often continued.

The installation of bases, shipbuilding and harbour facilities proved a boon to the Maltese economy. By 1880 the Grand Harbour in Valletta was a major entrepôt, with many ships calling at the port. Thereafter, however, as the size

The Language Dilemma
When the British arrived on the scene, the people's spoken language was Maltese, as it is today. But the knights had used Italian for official matters, and the middle and upper classes continued to use it, especially in the courts and for business. Sir Thomas Maitland declared that English should be used, but years of confusion followed before English was finally adopted as the official administrative language in 1921.

During British rule, English was taught in schools—as it has been since independence. Most Maltese speak good English.

of the ships became larger and outside investment declined, competition from other ports increased and Malta's importance as a centre of trade diminished.

During the 19th century, a succession of constitutions gave the Maltese varying degrees of autonomy. Then local riots in 1919 brought about changes, resulting in the new Constitution of 1921. The Maltese became responsible for their own internal affairs, with Great Britain, through its governor, retaining control of foreign affairs and imperial matters.

The Second Great Siege

Malta's finest hour in modern times was undoubtedly the heroic defence of the islands in World War II, which earned the George Cross. A vital Allied base, Malta was a haven for aircraft and ships. It not only helped to block the deployment of Italy's naval forces, but also threatened Axis supply routes between the European continent and the forces (above all, those under General Rommel) that were

Caravaggio's Beheading of St. John *adorns the oratory of St. John's Co-Cathedral in Valletta.*

operating in North Africa. It was no surprise, therefore, when Italian and Italian-based German bombers and fighters attacked Malta in 1941 in a fierce blitz that marked the start of a siege that was to last for months, until November 1942.

through to the beleaguered and suffering islands with a major convoy carrying urgently needed military and civilian supplies. This perilous operation was code-named "Pedestal".

In August 1942, fourteen supply ships and a tanker moved with naval and air cover through the straits of Gibraltar. There were a succession of fierce Italian air attacks on the convoy. Several ships were sunk and the tanker *Ohio*, a key ship, with its especially important cargo of oil, was badly damaged.

But despite a very rough five days of bombardment, on August 15th, the *Ohio* was finally towed into the Grand Harbour. The assembled crowds wept and cheered; Malta was saved. By November, when a major new Allied landing took place in Morocco and Rommel's forces were retreating from the frontiers of Egypt, following the battle of El Alamein, Malta could begin to see the victory that its own courage had helped make possible.

As Rommel advanced in Egypt in the spring of 1942, enemy air attacks were stepped up, and in March and April the islands were subjected to more than twice the weight of bombs falling in London during any year of the war.

That summer, life grew unbearably hard on Malta, and the people had to carry on in near-starvation conditions. The government in London therefore decided to take the huge risk of trying to force a way

But the price of freedom had been high: thousands of Maltese had been killed or seriously injured. It was only fitting, concluded Churchill, that Malta be awarded Great Britain's highest honour for civil courage—the George Cross.

Independence

In 1942, Great Britain provided Malta with £30 million towards reconstruction, and a new constitution granted the islands self-government within the Commonwealth. Malta attained full independence in 1964. It had a Governor-General and a Parliament of 50 members (now 65). In 1971, the Labour Party was voted into power with Dom Mintoff as Prime Minister.

The Union Jack was lowered for good on April 1, 1979. The occasion also marked the end of British financial aid and terminated years of friction between Britain and Dom Mintoff, who treated the withdrawal as Freedom Day. Under Labour party rule, Malta emphasized both a policy of neutrality and closer ties with communist countries and Libya and Algeria. But in 1987 the Nationalist party regained power. The new regime liberalized the economy, removed Arabic from the school curriculum, and strengthened links with the European Community.

Through all the upheavals, the Maltese never wavered in their goodwill towards the British residents on Malta and Gozo and the thousands of Britons who holiday there.

Where to Go

As the longest distance in Malta (from south-east to north-west) is only just over 16 miles, it is very easy to see a great deal in a short time. But quality is better than quantity, and the real advantage of Malta's tiny size is that you can take your time at places of interest and plan your sightseeing in any order you like, depending on whether you're in the mood for churches, villages, prehistoric sites, boat trips, beaches or just a shopping expedition in Valletta.

Thousands of years of dramatic history are compressed into these few square miles. You'll have to fight off many a tempting distraction if you hope to catch up with all the island's significant sights. In this book, we start with Valletta and suburbs, move on to Mdina and Rabat and then visit the south-east and north-west coasts. The special section on Malta's prehistoric temples gathers all the information on this ancient and mysterious culture into one chapter for handy reference. Finally, we give a complete summary of where to go on Gozo. But first, the city that has been at the centre of Malta's turbulent history...

MALTA

Valletta

"That splendid town, quite like a dream", wrote Sir Walter Scott. When you see Valletta, especially from the air or sea late on a dazzling summer's afternoon, you'll agree with him. The light plays games with the city's bright stone bastions and buildings, turning it into a place of enchantment that seems to float on an indigo sea.

It was not always this way. Mdina, the walled inland city, had been the capital of Malta from pre-Roman times until the Great Siege of 1565. But Grand Master Jean Parisot de la Valette saw the defensive possibilities of the Sceberras peninsula and his imagination was fired. After the knights' victory, plans were laid to build a capital town with invulnerable fortifications. The sharply hog-backed ridge with its two great natural harbours, Marsamxett on one side and the Grand Harbour on the other,

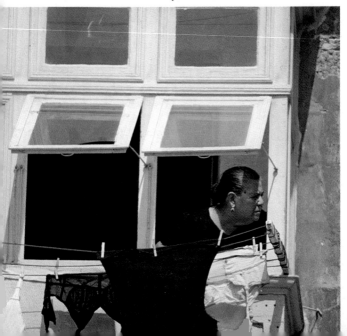

was the perfect place for a fortified town. So it was that in 1566, despite the enormous cost anticipated, work was begun by Francesco Laparelli, who had served as architect to Cosimo de' Medici and Pope Pius IV.

Laparelli is said to have masterminded the entire city plan in a mere three days, and two years later, when he left, Gerolamo Cassar (his Maltese assistant) took over and kept to the original conception.

The new city was constructed quickly but intelligently. Around the base, a solid line of stone curtains and bastions made it virtually impregnable. The uniformity of the grid-shaped street plan led it to be called a "city built for gentlemen". Water supply problems were solved in the 17th century

Woman in black, left, peers over laundry at Valletta life; flower stall adds colour and fragrance.

when Grand Master Alof de Wignacourt ordered the construction of an aqueduct to carry water from springs near Mdina to the new capital and gardens were added near the fortifications.

Valletta suffered from merciless bombing in World War II, but it was a victorious and courageous Maltese people who wept with joy when the blockade was broken in 1942. They are proud of their city, and have kept its original charms intact. It is a city with a soul, where everyone Maltese, from aristocrat to simple fisherman, walks with his head held high.

Around the Old Town

The best way to visit Valletta is on foot. Driving is inadvisable, as the streets are narrow and many are closed to traffic. Sunset is a good moment for a walk round, when shadows are cooling the streets, and the town is seething with strollers out for the evening social hour known as the *passeggiata*.

Enter the city after the roundabout bus terminal and Triton Fountain through the modern City Gate built in postwar style, with an arcade and complex of shops on either side. Directly ahead is the main Republic Street, formerly

Fortifications Galore

In the 16th century, one of the first things to be done after constructing a new city was to put up fortifications of one kind or another. Valletta, Floriana and their surrounding suburbs contain enough bastions, curtains, forts, towers, cavaliers, ravelins, ramparts, trenches, ditches, walls and other defensive structures to send any budding military engineer into frissons of ecstasy.

The typical zig-zag bastion provided the most effective defence. The nearer the enemy approached the bastion, the easier it became for the defenders to fire on the attackers along the flanks. Defences were thus "strengthened" without a real increase in arms, ammunition or men.

The best way to appreciate Valletta's fortifications (completed between 1566 and 1570) is to walk along the tops of them. To go around completely once takes about two hours (allowing for time to stop and admire the views).

called Kingsway. It is closed to all motor traffic. Parallel to it on the right is the second principal artery, Merchants Street. Both streets run straight on for just under a mile, to Fort St. Elmo at the end of the peninsula.

In Freedom Square, you'll see the sad ruins of the classical old opera house built by E. M. Barry—a grim reminder of the bombing in World War II. To the right is Valletta's oldest church, the Baroque **Our Lady of Victories,** completed in 1567 to commemorate the Great Siege victory. (Its front was remodelled in the 17th century.) Next to it a crumbling reddish façade is what remains of one of the earliest houses built in the city. Opposite is the church of St. Catherine of Italy, a domed structure originally designed by Cassar, but later rebuilt.

A few steps further on, you come to the **Auberge de Castile et Léon,** most impressive of the *auberges**, now containing the office of the Prime Minister. It is a magnificent ochre stone construction originally built to Cassar's design, but rebuilt by a Maltese architect (Dominico Cachia) for the Portuguese Grand Master Pinto in the 18th century. Unfortunately the public can see this elegant structure from the outside only.

Just beyond Castile place are the **Upper Barracca Gardens,** built in the 18th century. With green shrubs and trees,

* The *auberges* (inns) are the buildings where the knights were accommodated. Each *langue* had its own *auberge*.

bright hibiscus and statues, the area is a pleasant retreat where the knights used to stroll and supposedly hatch plots, or where people watched the knights set off on expeditions. Among the statues you'll see today are a group of children, *Les Gavroches*, by Antonio Sciortino, the Maltese sculptor, a big monument to Lord Strickland, Prime Minister from 1927 to 1930, a bust of Sir Winston Churchill and the inconspicuous tomb of Sir Thomas Maitland, "King Tom", the intransigent governor from 1813 to 1824.

From under the colonnade here, there's a stunning **view**

The Prime Minister's office is housed in Auberge de Castille (left); sculpture is by Sciortino.

across the Grand Harbour. On the far left is the 17th-century Fort Ricasoli; directly ahead is Fort St. Angelo (an important stronghold in the Great Siege) at Vittoriosa; to the right, in Dockyard Creek, is where the knights had their boats repaired. Further along is Senglea (see p. 44), behind which rises the little town of Cospicua (because it's conspicuous, the guides tell you). To the right of Senglea, across the creek, stands a modern grain silo. **33**

Finally, directly below, on Lascaris Wharf, is the old Customs House, attractively built in Venetian style.

Returning to Merchants Street, you'll see **Parisio Palace** on the right, where Napoleon stayed for a few days in 1798. Now the Ministry of Foreign Affairs, the palace is a sober 18th-century building. On the opposite side of the street, the Auberge d'Italie is an austere building built by Cassar in the 16th century and later modified. It is now the General Post Office.

Make your way from Merchants Street to **Republic Street** via Melita Street. This main thoroughfare is a real beehive of activity, with all kinds of shops, cafés, snack bars and pharmacies. The **Church of Santa Barbara** (between South Street and Melita Street) is unusual for its oval shape. This was the church used by the knights of the *langue* of Provence. The

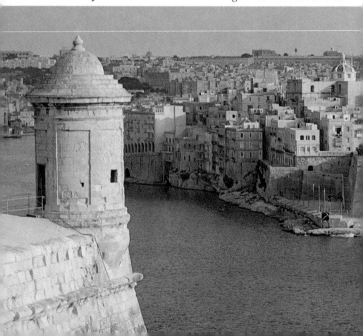

decor is simple; the Roman Catholic services are held in English, French and German.

Conveniently near to the church, the **Auberge de Provence,** on the left going towards Fort St. Elmo, now houses the excellent **National Museum of Archaeology** (for opening hours, see p. 117). This *auberge*, founded in 1571 and designed by Gerolamo Cassar, is symmetrical, with Doric columns below, Ionic above, and interesting "quoins" on ei-ther side of the building. Its façade was remodelled in the 17th century. After the knights left in 1798, the *auberge* was lived in by several different groups of people and served for many years as the Union Club.

The museum collection, put together in the 17th and 18th centuries and reorganized by

View from the bastions: Senglea and part of the dockyards.

Sir Themistocles Zammit, a famed Maltese scholar, was housed elsewhere until the inauguration of the museum in 1957.

It's essential to see this collection to better understand Malta's prehistoric sites. Some of the fascinating objects here are the famed small "Sleeping Woman" from the Hypogeum underground burial site, and the huge lower half of a "fat lady" transplanted from Tarxien, where she was getting eroded by the weather and elements. There are artifacts from all Malta's prehistoric periods, but some of the Tarxien ones are probably the most interesting—such as weapons and carbonized seeds, or a curious plate engraved with bulls and goats.

The shards of a few big bowls and vases from the Tarxien period have been reassembled. From the number found, it is thought that breaking vessels may have been part of the ancient religious cult.

Another exhibit, a case of skulls on the ground floor, shows the "long-heads" who were the first civilized Maltese settlers. These people disappeared completely later and were followed by settlers with differently shaped heads.

36 Upstairs, the museum

Of Palaces and Galleries

A large number of the palaces and noble buildings you'll see on Malta have rather blank, almost unfriendly façades. Privacy and security were of the utmost importance in the past and many buildings were entered only by an arched doorway on the side. Some palaces however have projecting and decorative stone balconies from the floor above the street level, with French doors opening onto them. In the inside of these palaces the plain architecture gives way to charming, sunny courtyards.

In Valletta, you'll also see many *galleriji* brightly painted wooden enclosed balconies. It was here that the strictly cloistered women of the past were able to get a glimpse of the outside world and, presumably, a breath of fresh air.

houses some interesting Roman and Punic (Carthaginian) items, especially two jewellery cases, and a *cippus* (small pillar) that has inscriptions in Phoenician and Greek on it, which enabled scholars to find the key for the deciphering of Phoenician. Its twin was given to Louis XIV and is now in the Louvre in Paris.

Several of the exhibits once on display at the National

Museum have been moved to the Fine Arts Museum.

After leaving the museum, if you turn down again towards Fort St. Elmo, you'll come to **St. John Square** and the Cathedral off to the right. A crafts centre is housed in a corner of the square and the neighbouring section of Merchants Street is an open-air market on weekday mornings. (On Sundays, it moves to St. James Ditch.)

St. John's Co-Cathedral (for opening hours, see p. 117), the knights' own church, was built from 1573 to 1577 to the plans of Gerolamo Cassar. It's considered to be his masterpiece and was raised to cathedral status in 1816 by Pope Pius VII. It's called "co-" because it shares the distinction with Mdina Cathedral.

Financed by funds contributed by Grand Master de la Cassière, who after the Great Siege was very keen to have all religious activity transferred from Birgu to Valletta as quickly as possible, the church has a rather heavy façade, which isn't likely to make you gasp with admiration. However, the interior reveals a staggering display of Baroque art. This elaborate production should be savoured at some length. Sir Walter Scott wrote

that he had never seen a more striking church nave. The barrel-vaulted space is 189 feet long, 64 feet high and 115 feet wide. Everything in the enormous structure leads the eye up to the high altar. On both sides the nave is flanked with **chapels**, most of which were built by the various *langues* of the knights and named after saints. Every square inch of this church is carved in high relief with brightly painted religious motifs as sumptuous as a Rubens painting. Plenty of gilt touches add to the rich effect.

The polychrome marble paving on the floor covers the tombstones of the knights and is decorated with coats of arms, trophies, skeletons, and so on.

On the right-hand side of the nave, you'll see the chapels of St. James, St. George, St. Sebastian and the Blessed Sacrament. This last one has an extraordinary **screen** and **gates** in solid silver, which, legend says, were cleverly concealed by being painted black when the French were on a pillaging spree in their 1798 stay.

The vault of the church is decorated with oil-on-stone **paintings** by the 17th-century Calabrian painter Mattia Preti. The pictures tell the story of the life of St. John the Baptist, **37** and took the artist five years (1662–67) to complete.

The rich **high altar** (1681) was designed by architect Lorenzo Gafà, and presents an elaborate array of marble, silver-plate and lapis lazuli. The group behind the altar is of the Baptism of Christ, by Sicilian sculptor Giuseppe Mazzuoli.

The crypt, entered from the Chapel of Provence, may be visited on request between 10 a.m. and 12 noon; it contains the tombs of the first twelve Grand Masters.

Going back towards the entrance you'll see on the right the chapels of St. Charles (or of the Holy Relics), St. Michael,

St. Paul, St. Catherine and the Chapel of the Magi. Most chapels have busts or other monuments commemorating almost all the Grand Masters. In the sacristy there are paintings by Stefano Pieri, Preti and Antoine de Favray.

To reach the **oratory and museum,** take a door on the right facing the altar, third bay from the entrance. The oratory's main feature is the monumental painting by Caravaggio, *The Beheading of St. John,* widely esteemed to be the fin-

Horse-drawn karrozzin, *one way to see sights of historic Valletta.*

est painting in Malta. Commissioned by the Grand Master to paint several works, Caravaggio ended up by assaulting one of the knights. The details of the story are unclear but the artist left the country in disgrace in 1608. The painting is a rather lurid work, but dramatically moving, with good use of chiaroscuro and lively Baroque composition.

The museum contains the impressive Judocus de Vos **tapestries** which are hung out in the church nave in June. The 17th-century works are based on religious paintings by Rubens and Poussin.

Back on Republic Street and continuing towards Fort St. Elmo, you'll come to **Great Siege Square.** The square has a powerful allegorical monument by Sciortino. Opposite are the new Law Courts, a neo-classic colonnaded building, on the site of the Auberge d'Auvergne, bombed out in World War II.

Republic Square, also off Republic Street, has a spacious outdoor café and little shops under the shady arcades.

At the back of the square is the **National Library.** Once the Library of the Order (and later the Royal Malta Library), it was constructed in the late 18th century mainly to house the large collection amassed by the knights. The archives of the Order include documents dating back to the 11th century.

From Republic Square, you can go through a big Baroque archway into the first courtyard of the **Grand Master's Palace** (Magisterial Palace), now the seat of the House of Representatives. In 1569, the nephew of Grand Master del Monte built a large house here—probably the first private house in Valletta—and later the knights commissioned Gerolamo Cassar to enlarge the building into a palace. Today some parts house museums.

You'll find two cool, green courtyards in the palace grounds, one of them called Neptune Court, after its statue and the other, Prince Alfred's Court (the one nearest Republic Square). Look out for the **clock** installed by Grand Master Pinto de Fonseca (1741–73), with little figures gonging the hours.

To visit the palace, take the staircase from Prince Alfred Courtyard. In the council chamber, formerly the meeting-place of Malta's Parliament, you can sit on one of the heavy bench-seats and admire the beautiful Gobelins **tapestries** given to the Order by

Grand Master Ramon Perellos in the early 18th century. Called *Les Tentures des Indes,* they represent all kinds of real and fanciful beasts and birds, with exotically clad Indians.

The grandest of the various public rooms is the **Hall of St. Michael and St. George,** or Throne Room, with a beamed ceiling and frieze by Matteo Perez d'Aleccio. Scenes of the Great Siege fill the walls, and the carved gallery comes from the ship in which Villiers de l'Isle Adam sailed away from Rhodes in 1523.

The damask-hung **Hall of Ambassadors** or Red Room features heavy and dark portraits of famous notables: Louis XIV by De Troy, Louis XV by Van Loo, Catherine II of Russia by Levitsky—a rather unfortunate rendering of that imposing monarch.

The **Armoury,** upstairs in the Palace, is notable for its immense collection of suits of mail; especially striking is the gold-inlaid **ceremonial suit** made for Grand Master Alof de Wignacourt, and some captured Turkish arms, including, it's said, the corsair Dragut's sword.

Leaving the palace by the Neptune Court archway, you'll see the Greek Catholic Church on Archbishop Street

The Hospital of the Order
The splendid buildings and halls of the Mediterranean Conference Centre started as the hospital of the knights in 1574.

The knights took in anyone of any faith who was ill and treated the sick as *seigneurs malades* (sick lords) with respect and humility. The standard of medical treatment was high and the patients were given good food served on silver dishes. All the knights, from the youngest novices to the Grand Master, served the patients.

The hospital was taken over by the French when they occupied Malta and later by the British. During the war, the buildings were badly damaged by bombs.

—unremarkable except for a 12th-century **icon** called Our Lady of Damascus, which the knights brought with them when they came to Malta in 1530. It was well restored in 1966.

Just a few steps away is the **Gesù Church,** built between 1592 and 1600, richly ornate in Italian Baroque style.

Take Merchants' Street down to the **Mediterranean Conference Centre.** The restoration of the badly bombed-out former **41**

Shipwrecked St. Paul inspires a cool, dark bar in Valletta street.

hospital of the Order is one of independent Malta's finest achievements. Opened in 1979, the centre contains six conference rooms as well as the beautiful 520-foot-long hall that was once the Great Ward in the old hospital.

A must for any first-time visitor to Malta is the documentary film *The Malta Experience.* It's an excellent introduction to the history of the islands. Headphones carry the commentary in six languages.

Star-shaped **Fort St. Elmo,** occupies the whole of the end of the peninsula. You can only enter the main part with permission from the police headquarters. However, you can visit the **National War Museum** of World War II relics: *Faith,* one of the four Gladiator bi-planes that were Malta's air defence when Italy declared war in 1940; *Husky,* the jeep used by General Eisenhower and later President Roosevelt; and the George Cross conferred on Malta and the Maltese people in 1942 for their courage under bombardment. (For opening hours, see p. 117.)

Other Places of Interest

Proceeding back towards City Gate via Spur and Fountain streets, you'll come to Strait Street (also known as the Gut), a narrow, colourful and notorious lane which still has the bars and hangouts that have given it a reputation among sailors for low life. This street was the only place the knights were allowed to fight duels.

Close by is Independence Square, with a pretty view through to Marsamxett harbour. On the right you'll see the **Auberge d'Aragon**, the first *auberge* built in Valletta in the 16th century, with a Doric porch added later. Opposite, St. Paul's Anglican Cathedral was constructed in neo-classical style in the 19th century and paid for by the Dowager Queen Adelaide after a visit to Malta in 1838–39. Its 200-foot **bell tower** is a striking landmark.

The **Carmelite Church** on Old Theatre Street is another landmark. Its huge dome is 138 feet high. Severely bombed in the war, this larger church has now been rebuilt over the ruins of the old one.

The **Manoel Theatre,** built in 1731 under the rule of Grand Master Manoel de Vilhena, is a lovely 18th-century creation, one of Europe's oldest theatres still in use. At one time, the theatre underwent an unfortunate period of decay, but it is now restored as Malta's National Theatre and is a gem, with its neat, oval shape, tiered, gilded and painted boxes. Tours begin at the box office in Old Theatre Street—see p. 117 for times.

There are several other Baroque churches to see in the old city, such as St. Roque and St. Ursula (both in St. Ursula Street) and **St. Paul Shipwrecked,** in St. Paul Street. This is a rich-looking 18th-century church with a 19th-century façade. Its outstanding treasure is a Baroque **statue of St. Paul,** carved by Melchiorre Gafà.

The **National Museum of Fine Arts** is on South Street, which crosses Republic Street up near City Gate. The building is an attractive white palace (16th century, later restored), built around a sunny courtyard, where contemporary exhibits are shown in the summer. Once used by the knights, it later served as the official residence of the Commander-in-Chief of the British Mediterranean Fleet.

The **collection** (most of which came from the National Museum of Archaeology) contains paintings from various periods of the Italian, Flemish and Dutch schools plus later compositions by French artists Antoine de Favray, Claude Joseph Vernet and Louis de Cros. There are also some fine works of the 20th-century Maltese sculptor Antonio Sciortino.

The basement exhibit revives memories of the knights' hospital work, with vases, apothecary vessels and the famous elaborate **silverware** from which the knights served their patients.

Near City Gate (off to the right before you exit) are **Hastings Gardens,** named after the Marquess of Hastings, Governor of Malta from 1824 to 1826, whose funerary statue reposes in the gardens. From here there is a splendid **view** of Marsamxett Harbour—with Floriana, St. Publius Church and Independence Arena on the far left. You can also appreciate the huge **bastions** of St. Michael's and St. Andrew's here. They were built up after the Great Siege and are 60 to 70 feet thick. Across the way are Msida and Lazzaretto creeks, then Manoel Island, Dragut Point and Tigné Fort.

Walking back to City Gate before taking a staircase down, you'll cross the fortifications of St. James' Cavalier and St. John's Cavalier (the latter presently the knights' embassy in Malta).

Around Valletta

Floriana

Any approach to Valletta by land inevitably goes through the spacious Floriana area, named after Paolo Floriani, the Italian military engineer who recommended that Valletta be protected by outer fortresses on the land approach.

Here you'll drive under or beside the **Porte des Bombes,** a double arched gateway, one arch built in the 18th century, another built for aesthetic balance by the British. On St. Anne Street are the British and American embassies. St. Publius Church is a handsome two-towered building of the 18th century, named after Malta's first bishop. In an attractive garden setting nearby is the Phoenicia Hotel, the island's grandest old hostelry, a classic example of "British Colonial" style.

Vittoriosa, Senglea, Cospicua

Just on the other side of the Grand Harbour from Valletta are "the three cities", which you can reach by bus from City Gate, or after a pleasant, short ride in a *dgħajsa* (water taxi) from Customs House wharf (agree on a price in advance), or by car via Marsa.

At the heart of **Vittoriosa,** in Majjistral (or Mistral) Street, is the pretty façade of the Auberge d'Angleterre. Nearby, the diminutive church on the lower left side of Vittoriosa Square is called St. Joseph's. You can ask for a key at the "museum" door around the corner— though there is not much to see inside except for a sword and hat belonging to Jean de la Valette.

Past a quiet square is the **Church of St. Lawrence,** originally the knights' Conventual Church before the move to Valletta. It was re-built by Romano Carapecchia in 1691 and is richly decorated inside with paintings and pink marble columns. Outside, a plaque records the death of Sir Nicholas Upton, who fell defending Malta from the Turks in 1551. Another plaque commemorates the dead killed after bombing in World War II, when the church's dome was destroyed.

Below the church is a new Freedom Monument, unveiled on March 31, 1979, when the British Navy finally left for good: a British sailor shakes hands with a Maltese dock-worker. The blue-painted buildings you'll see here were the Royal Navy's bakeries; now they are government property.

Fort St. Angelo, now a tourist complex, has an excellent view of the Grand Harbour, and was already built on in Phoenician times with, it is thought, a temple to Astarte, followed by a Greek temple to Hera and a Roman one to Juno. Within the fort, the Saint Anne chapel has a reputedly classical column. The fort was the Royal Navy's headquarters during World War II, and held up well, considering the number of times it was bombed.

Senglea and Cospicua were both heavily bombed in World War II, and have been re-built in rather uninspired modern style as suburban residential areas. SENGLEA, also called l'Isla, was named after the Grand Master who fortified it before the Great Siege, Claude

After the Great Siege, triumphant knights named town Vittoriosa. **47**

The Harbour by Boat

These conducted two-hour boat tours leaving from Sliema are excellent for a sea view of Valletta and environs. Various companies run the trips several times daily. A guide explains exactly what you're looking at, and you'll see things like the place where the knights put huge chains across the Grand Harbour to keep the Turks out, the wharves of the Grand Harbour Marina and big cruise-ships from Norway, Italy or Greece.

In one of the "creeks" are huge tankers, in another you'll see the dry dockyard project, built with the help of the People's Republic of China; the looming 95-foot-high crane here is one of the world's largest, capable of lifting 150 tons. There are many more romantic vistas, however, including Valletta itself from the sea—a majestic group of fortresses, spires and domes.

de la Sengle. At Isola Point, it has a pretty little garden and a look-out post sculpted aptly with an eye and an ear. Cospicua (also known as Bormla), is ringed by the formidable walls of the **Cotonera lines,** named after 17th-century Grand Master Cotoner.

Sliema and St. Julian's Bay

These are the lively high spots of Malta for hotels, nightlife and shopping.

Sliema, a thriving suburb of 24,000 people, is a lot larger than Valletta. It's about 3 miles from Floriana to Sliema's Strand, passing by or through the districts of Pieta, Msida and Ta' Xbiex, none of them particularly pretty.

Sliema is quite new and has grown fast in recent years. Its general appearance might

Dynamic tourist zone surrounds quiet village of St. Julian's Bay.

best be described as undistinguished. Yet it has good shops, restaurants, hotels, and suitable flat spots along the rocky shoreline for swimming.

After St. Julian's Point with its fortified tower, now a pleasant café, you reach BALLUTTA BAY, and round the corner **St. Julian's Bay,** a quaint old fishing village that has several shops and a couple of good café-restaurants. Just a bit further along, before ST. GEORGE'S BAY, are some luxury hotels,

seaside discos and the Casino. The entire area swarms with bathers on summer weekends.

Slightly inland, ST. ANDREW'S, once a huge military base with its own shops, banks and churches, is now gradually being converted into a tourist complex. **49**

Inland to Mdina and Rabat

Mdina is about 7 miles from Valletta, through busy HAMRUN, an industrial suburb. The road passes by the **aqueduct** built in the 17th century by Grand Master Wignacourt to bring water into Valletta.

Off to the right from ATTARD, you might want to take a detour to the **San Anton Gardens.** This is a refreshing, shady spot with exotic subtropical trees and flowers, some giant evergreens—possibly descendants of the islands' lusher days millenia ago when lots of rain and greenery brought abundant wildlife—and a mini-zoo. The dignified, bougainvillea- and ivy-covered house at the opposite end of the gardens is the official residence of the President of Malta; it was built in the 17th century by Grand Master Antoine de Paule.

Further along the road, also branching off to the right, is TA 'QALI, a former airfield converted in 1972 into a crafts village (see p. 88).

Mdina

This historic citadel is one of Malta's most beautiful spots, a must for any visitor. The old city stands out like a splendid ship's prow at an altitude of 700 feet overlooking the plains and hills to the sea. It may have been inhabited since the Bronze Age, but in any case there were Punic and Roman settlements here. The Romans called it *Melita* (honey); St. Publius, the Roman governor converted by St. Paul and first bishop of Malta, lived here. When the Saracens fortified the promontory in the 9th century, they re-named it *Mdina* (the city) and separated it from its "suburb", Rabat.

Also known as Città Notabile, Mdina was the first capital of Malta, dating back to before Roman times. Later it was the Bishop's See and seat of the Università, the government advisory body. It was in Mdina that Roger the Norman was hailed as the island's liberator from the Arabs in 1090. When the knights decided that Valletta would be a better capital, Mdina became Città Vecchia (old city).

Now Mdina is known as "the silent city", intriguing and secretive within its narrow, nearly deserted streets. Its air of mystery is enhanced by the fact that several of Malta's aristocratic old families still live here—very discreetly in enclosed palaces.

To enter the city, there are

two large gates (both dated 1724) past the Howard Gardens and a bridged-over moat. The left gate is Greeks' Gate. Take the main **Mdina Gate** on the right. Just inside you'll see the harmonious courtyard and façade of a palace built in French style, **Vilhena Palace** (named after the Grand Master who had it built in the 18th century). It currently houses a quaint Museum of Natural History, whose most interesting exhibit is a three-dimensional display showing the geological "sandwich" of Malta and Gozo's rock formations. Across from the palace is the 16th-century Torre dello Standardo,

now the police station. **Villegaignon Street** is the town's main thoroughfare and runs straight through to the fortified edge of town.

To the right is the Convent of St. Benedict, a blank-walled building where no men are admitted. The two small churches are St. Peter's and St. Agatha's. On the left you'll see **Casa Inguanez,** the palace home of Malta's oldest titled family; the main entrance is around on Mesquita, a side street. The door is typical, with a good pair of brass Neptune knockers. Testaferrata Palace just off St. Paul's Square is an imposing building with a collection

1 Church of the Annunciation
2 St. Roque
3 Palazzo Santa Sophia
4 Casa del Magistrato
5 Banca Giuratale
6 Archbishop's Palace
7 Cathedral Museum
8 St. Nicolas' Chapel
9 Palazzo Gatto-Murina
10 Casa Viani
11 Testaferrata Palace
12 Casa Inguanez
13 St. Peter's
14 St. Agatha's Chapel
15 Convent of St. Benedict
16 Torre dello Standardo
17 Vilhena Palace and Natural History Museum
18 Roman Villa and Museum

MDINA

MOSTA

Bastion Sq.
Norman House
Carmel St.
St. Peter St.
St. Sophia St.
Holy Cross
Magazine Street
Nicolas Street
St. Paul's Square
St. Roque St.
Villegaignon Street
Bastion Street
DE REDIN BASTION
Cathedral
Archbishop Square
Gatto-Murina Street
Mesquita Street
St. Paul Street
Greeks' Gate
Inguanez Street
Xara Palace
Mdina Gate
N

MTARFA
MGARR
Mtarfa Road
Museum Esplanade
Howard Gardens
Museum Rd.
MOSTA

PARISH SQUARE,
ST. PAUL'S GROTTO & CATACOMBS,
ST. AGATHA'S CATACOMBS

VERDALA CASTLE,
BUSKETT

ST. AUGUSTINE'S
CHURCH

0   50   100   150 m
0   50   100   150 yards

of art but not open to the public.

The striking **cathedral** (seat of the bishopric and "co-cathedral" with St. John's in Valletta) is outstanding as a Baroque work on an island already abounding in Baroque art. Fronted by a pair of cannon, flanked by its two bell towers, it has three doorways with two types of pilasters (Corinthian below, composite above), making an admirable façade when seen from the other end of the square.

The first church was built some time in the 13th century—according to legend, on the site of the house belonging to Publius. But all except the apse was destroyed by an earthquake in 1693. The new cathedral was built between 1697 and 1702 by Lorenzo Gafà and is considered his masterwork. The interior, under an impressive dome, is well-proportioned, yet very rich, especially the colourful floor—whose marble mosaic surface covers the tombs of bishops.

Noteworthy items to see in the cathedral: the heavy wooden **doors** through the vestry, carved with snakes and other motifs; a lively **fresco,** *The Shipwreck of St. Paul* by Mattia Preti, in the apse; to the left of the apse, a silver **processional cross,** brought to Malta (according to tradition) by the knights from Rhodes.

Just to the right of the Archbishop's Palace, outside the Cathedral, the former semina-

Mdina's cathedral boasts a Baroque façade worthy of the name.

ry now houses the **Cathedral Museum.** It contains much that was saved from the old cathedral, including exquisite 15th-century marquetry from the old choir, the bishop's carriage and various papal bulls. There are also Punic and Roman remains. The outstanding **coin collection** will thrill any numismatist and intrigue others; it is beautifully displayed in mirrored cases, to take you from Carthage all the way through to modern Europe, with a stop at many historical moments.

Upstairs is a collection of paintings from various schools (Sicilian, Flemish, Spanish, 16th–18th centuries), and an excellent group of Dürer woodcuts, plus engravings by Rembrandt, Piranesi, Van Dyck and Goya. And you might want to glance at a collection of beautiful illuminated choirbooks dating from the 11th century, as well as some valuable silver religious objects in another room.

Further along Villegaignon Street is the **Palazzo Santa Sophia,** reputedly the oldest house in Mdina, with a typical Maltese feature—a "string-course" of triangular corbels with balls attached to them.

The **Church of the Annunciation** is the next big building on the left; its bells played a **53** part in the 1798 revolt. The French wanted to sell the valuable tapestries belonging to the church, but after an incident when a young boy attacked the French Commandant Masson, the bells were rung to call people from the neighbouring countryside. After a good deal of brawling, the enraged Maltese threw Commandant Masson to his death from the balcony of the notary's house. This was one of the first actions in the rebellion that would last until the French were ousted in 1800.

Near the end of Villegaignon Street on the right is the **Norman house,** or the Palazzo Falzon. The lower part was the earliest section of the house, a defensive façade with only slits for windows (14th-15th centuries). The later upper section has attractive double-arched windows.

At the end of the street, you'll come to a large bastion with a magnificent **view,** extending out to Mosta with its big red dome, all the way to the spires of Valletta in the east.

If you return to the cathedral via Bastion Street, to the left and parallel to Villegaignon Street, you might stop at a café for a drink and a sweeping view over south-east Malta.

Rabat

Before reaching Rabat, past Howard Gardens, you'll find the **Roman villa and museum** worth visiting. This small columned building in pinkish stone, garlanded by rhododendron, has been nicely restored. Inside, you can see remains from Greek, Carthaginian and Roman tombs. Downstairs in the atrium are some finely-drawn original mosaics. The technique is called "vermiculatum". The most amusing ones show two naiads beating up a satyr, and an elegant bird drinking out of a goblet.

Rabat itself is Mdina's suburb and contains both old and modern buildings. **St. Augustine's Church** on St. Augustine Street was built by Cassar, two years before Valletta's cathedral, and it foreshadows St. John's—especially the massive barrel-vaulted interior.

In the heart of Rabat on Parish Square is **St. Paul's Church** —a rich 16th-century building that some think was at least partly the work of Lorenzo Gafà, notably the big dome. The church at festival time (late June, early July) displays a particularly rich array of scarlet damask, 12-foot-high silver candlesticks and other valuables. The square outside, too, is exuberantly decorated.

In Rabat, islanders venerate St. Paul's Grotto, where the apostle is said to have sheltered for an entire winter in the 1st century A.D.

Just outside the church (on the left, downstairs) is **St. Paul's Grotto.** You can pay a few cents to have the cave lit where St. Paul supposedly sheltered when he was in Malta. Legend has it that no matter how much stone is extracted from the cave, by some miracle it always "grows" back.

The **catacombs** (St. Paul's and St. Agatha's; signs point there) are cool, maze-like galleries and passageways. The size suggests that a large Christian community lived in the area in the 4th and 5th centuries. The circular platforms are thought to be stone tables used for funeral feasts, and in some of the chambers prayers may have been held.

Verdala, Buskett, Dingli

Take the road from Rabat to Buskett, and **Verdala Castle** lies just east off the road, a few minutes from Rabat. It is open on Tuesdays and Fridays, with excellent tours conducted by the caretaker/curator, and well worth a visit inside and out. Once the summer residence of Grand Masters and Governors, it is now an official guest-house for important visitors. Gerolamo Cassar built this square castle surrounded by a moat and pine groves in 1586 as the summer residence of Grand Master de Verdalle, Cardinal Verdala. It has a magnificent **staircase** offering vast views.

The **Buskett** or Boschetto (meaning little wood) is Malta's most fertile green area, the spot where the knights raised their falcons for hunting. On June 28th and 29th, Malta's famed folklore festival is held here, and the quiet grove hums with singing and dancing.

The Inquisitor's summer palace, built in the 17th century, is a charming setting for such an awe-inspiring individual, who no doubt found the verdant surroundings a good place to relax from his weighty duties. Although recently restored, it is not open to visitors. Driving back via the south roads, you'll pass through a tiny village, DINGLI, and then over to the **Dingli Cliffs,** where you can enjoy a dizzying view of the sea from far above; over to the left is the tiny speck of Filfla island, made even smaller during and after World War II. (It was used by the British for bombing practice.)

South-East Coast

GĦAR LAPSI is a picturesque little village in a sheltered bay under the cliffs. Although the beach is small, the Maltese like to swim here. There are a few simple restaurants.

Further along, by the road that goes to ŻURRIEQ, is the **Blue Grotto**—not as large (or crowded) as the one in Capri, but some prefer this one. The approach road offers some spectacular views and leads to a small car-park, where you'll find a group of fishermen in their colourfully painted water taxis ready to shuttle you around the point and into the limestone caves. Try to go in the morning before 11, because this is when the light slants into the caves to reflect off the sheer white sand bottom. In some places your hand will literally glow a tasteful turquoise blue if you drag it in the water.

The 25-minute excursion takes in several caves, about which the fishermen give a little talk in English. The first cave is around 25 feet deep. It is tinted with lovely hues of pink, mauve and orange by coral and minerals in the limestone; you'll see the same effect in all three or four caves you visit, especially one called "Reflection Cave". The Blue Grotto itself could not be a more luminescent, pure blue, and coming out you'll see a square natural "window" in the rock, giving a fluorescent lamp effect.

Marsaxlokk on the eastern part of MARSAXLOKK BAY, is also known by the Italianized name Marsascirocco. It's Malta's largest fishing village, and with the calm blue water, bobbing *luzzu* boats, and the fishermen mending their red

Marsaxlokk housewife makes bags for souvenirs instead of fishnets.

nets, it's both colourful and genuinely peaceful. There are two similar baylets within the larger bay—ST. GEORGE'S BAY and PRETTY BAY, which were once favourite haunts of well-off Maltese, though some industry and modern installations have made Pretty Bay less worthy of its name.

Dragut the pirate landed in Marsaxlokk in 1565 and in the 17th century several defensive towers were built, still in evidence. But this didn't put off Napoleon, whose troops disembarked here in 1798. A small road running down to Delimara Point takes you first past Tas-Silġ Chapel, where there is a Carmelite Monastery, and the site of a Punic-Roman temple considered to be dedicated to Astarte or Hera. DELIMARA BAY and PETER'S POOL offer deep water rock swimming—a good way to escape beach crowds. At XROBB IL-GHA-ĠIN are some rather poor vestiges of a Neolithic temple.

Marsaskala, at the head of its own narrow bay, is much like a smaller Marsaxlokk, with its pastel houses and colourful fishing boats. Rapid building in recent years has lined the inlet with apartments and villas, and, where it meets the sea, one of Malta's biggest **58** resort hotels.

The North-West

Although relatively fertile, this part of Malta was difficult to defend in the past, so it was sparsely populated. Now, its handful of sandy beaches are a big attraction.

As you're heading this way, you will hardly miss one of the island's outstanding landmarks, the **dome** of the parish church in the busy little town of **Mosta.** The church, **St. Mary's,** was financed and built with local money and by voluntary labour between 1833 to 1860 to the design of architect Giorgio de Vassé, and the inhabitants are justly proud of it. The enormous **dome,** nearly 123 feet in diameter, was built without scaffolding, and is still one of the largest in the world. St. Mary's has a classical colonnaded façade, and the impression inside is one of "all dome", surrounded by apses. The geometrical marble floor heightens the dome effect. On the left side near the altar, a bomb fell through the dome on April 9, 1942, sliding across the floor with-

Getting around in traditional style: donkey carts and fishing boats serve the purpose admirably.

out exploding—a miracle for those present. Today you can view a replica of the bomb in the sacristy on the left.

North-west from Sliema and St. Julian's, **St. Andrew's,** once a huge army base, is now civilian housing and holiday facilities. The road hits the coast again at Bahar ic-Cagħaq, where there's a water slide park. After several headlands and old towers, you'll arrive at **Salina Bay,** with a John F. Kennedy Memorial Grove and small playground, salt pans and reedbeds. Further round the bay at **Qawra** (remember—the Q is almost silent), big resort hotels and beach clubs offer all water sports facilities.

Next, by rounding Qawra Point, where the knights' fort is now a restaurant, or by cutting across the peninsula, you'll reach **St. Paul's Bay.** On its south side, **Buġibba** village and the town of San Pawl il-Bahar have grown together into a major holiday resort, with water sports and swimming from the rocks or small sandy beaches. Hotels, apartments, restaurants, bars and discos have sprung up, but traditional life continues too, in the old parts of the town and the fishing harbour.

St. Paul came ashore near here after his shipwreck in A.D. 60; legend says it was on the larger of the two islands that you can see over the water.

Just near the innermost curve of the bay at GĦAJN RASUL (which means "apostle's fountain") is the fountain said to be on the spot where St. Paul struck a rock which miraculously brought forth water.

MISTRA BAY (a small bay within St. Paul's) is worth a short excursion. Following a road through Kalkara Ravine and a typical country landscape, you take a dirt road up to the redoubt which affords a grand **view;** the building was once a storage battery for the knights' artillery.

Dominating the countryside for miles around, the massive dome of the "village" church at Mġarr, built in 1927, is modelled on the one at Mosta.

Landmarks on Mellieħa Ridge above splendid but crowded beach.

Mellieħa Bay, just under Marfa Ridge (which is the "tail" of fish-shaped Malta), is the most beautiful stretch of sandy beach on Malta, and it's very likely to be crowded in season.

Up the hill on Mellieħa Ridge, perched on a commanding spur, MELLIEĦA itself (a small town of 4,000 inhabitants) offers a superb **view** of Marfa Ridge, Comino and Gozo with its bell-towers in the distance. To the left of Marfa Ridge is the Red Tower, built by the knights in 1649. Halfway down to the beach, beyond the red and white oleanders, you'll see a spruced-up cave house, originally made as a bomb shelter in World War II.

Mellieħa's reddish stone 18th-century **church** stands proudly like a fortress on the promontory, though nestled in it is a chapel from the early

Middle Ages, now a site of pilgrimage. Within the shrine is a small chapel with marble walls containing a **painting** of the Virgin said to be by St. Luke.

The northern shore of Marfa Ridge has several bays (some with sand) and swimming places, though the best-maintained is probably at **Ramla Bay,** with the modern hotel there. At Ċirkewwa is the landing place for the smaller, 20-minute ferry to Gozo.

The next bay is rocky but beautiful **Anchor Bay,** so named because it once had lots of large anchors on the shore.

Children will be overjoyed to find that the ramshackle **village** on the shore of Anchor Bay was in fact constructed as the set for the film *Popeye* and has been retained as a tourist attraction. A small admission fee is charged, and a shop sells Popeye souvenirs.

Golden Bay *(Ramla Tal-Mixquqa)* is edged with a golden crescent of sand, though it's not always pristine-clean. It is well-provided with hotels and cafés, and in the vicinity is a big tourist complex. Għajn Tuffieħa Bay next-door is approached via a long staircase, and attracts fewer swimmers than Golden Bay.

The Prehistoric Sites

Malta's prehistory is impressive and enigmatic. It all began with a wave of agricultural immigrants who came over from Sicily between 5000 and 4000 B.C. Successive migrations followed and have now been classified into various periods and names that you'll encounter in the sites and museums.

The different phases of Maltese prehistoric civilization are known as the Għar Dalam period, lasting to about 4500 B.C.*; the Skorba phase, 4500–4100 B.C., characterized by its grey and red pottery; Żebbuġ (3900 B.C.); Mġarr (3700 B.C.) and Ġgantija (around 3600–3000 B.C.). Outstanding in this latter period are the temples at Ġgantija on Gozo (see p.77), Ħaġar Qim, an early temple at Tarxien and a temple at Mnajdra. The Hal Saflieni Hypogeum at Paola is a remarkable complex dating back to perhaps 3300 B.C. The Tarxien period (around 3200–2500 B.C.) also

---

*All prehistoric dates must be regarded as approximate. Those quoted here agree with the latest available research, including the technique of dendrochronology, tree-ring dating, which gives dates substantially earlier than the results from carbon-14 testing, hitherto accepted.

Prehistoric Economics

How were the tombs and temples of ancient Malta produced and financed? This is a question that many archaeologists have asked themselves. The evidence suggests that the islanders lived peaceably together without trouble from outside neighbours. There was more rainfall thousands of years ago, so agriculture provided enough for the primitive people's needs.

A tribal system with tithes to the chief would have made it possible to achieve a structured society, able to pay priests and artisans, as well as providing organized labour to construct temples.

But the people must have imported flint and obsidian to be used as tools in their building, as these were not locally available. How they paid for these imports is still unsolved; though the medium of exchange may well have been something perishable, probably textiles and possibly even elaborate temple robes.

left behind very impressive temples.

Then came an unexplained complete break (around 2500 B.C.) in the temple-building civilization. Drought and starvation, emigration and mass suicide are a few of the speculations put forward.

The next group of immigrants used Tarxien as a cemetery from 2500 to 1500 B.C. and are called the Cemetery People. About 1500 B.C., came the Borg in-Nadur (Bronze Age) period, with a settlement at Borg in-Nadur. This was the last group of migrants until the Phoenicians in about 800 B.C.

Few hard facts are known about the type of religion practised by the temple-builders. Archaeologists have come up with a hypothetical cult related to both death and fertility. The presence of the huge, fat and skirted figure at Tarxien (the original is in the National Museum) would seem to suggest a fertility cult. A small terracotta "sleeping fat lady" (also in the National Museum) might be some sort of hope-prayer figure, or possibly a prophetess whose dreams had significance. There were also phallic symbols.

The construction of the temples was usually along the following lines. The curved outer walls were made of coralline limestone (a very hard limestone) with face or edge of blocks alternately projecting. Then came a packing of rubble and inner walls, usually of glo-

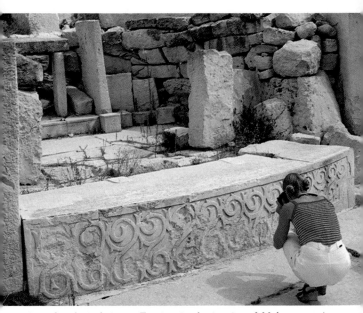

At archaeological site at Tarxien, in the interior of Malta, a tourist snaps bas-relief carvings of mysterious sect's prehistoric temple.

bigerina limestone. The final roof-hole was covered with wood and/or brush. Doorways and passages were erected on the trilithon principle—which resembles post and lintel.

Most temples were built in series of lobes around a central court or passage; temples had three, four, five or six lobes or apses. Common features in-cluded sacrificial altars, pos-sible "oracle chambers" and hollowed stones, perhaps for collecting sacrificial animal blood. Most temples were built behind a massive, concave entry wall.

Temple interiors and altars were decorated with carvings; and, though it seems hard to believe, the carving must have **65** been done with stone, since no metal tools have been found to correspond with this type of building. It's probable that simple colouring was used, too, although it hasn't survived thousands of years of weathering. Traces can still be seen in the Hypogeum.

During the Bronze Age, quite sophisticated metal-working techniques came to the islands, but the new race of immigrants produced nothing comparable to the earlier achievements, many of which pre-date other ancient wonders such as the Great Pyramid and Stonehenge. But the Maltese construction

techniques are unrelated to these, and considered unique. It would seem the builders learned nothing from elsewhere, and invented everything themselves.

The following are some of the more interesting sites and caves to be visited. Go with a qualified guide if possible.

About 6 miles from Valletta, **Ghar Dalam** is an important archaeological site. A small museum there shows the types of animals that existed on Malta in the Pleistocene era—such as hippopotamuses and dwarf elephants. At one time the sea covered Malta, then receded greatly, probably leaving a land bridge to Sicily, by which the large animals made the crossing. As the climate grew drier, and food became scarcer, the number of animals dwindled. Their bones and, later, human remains were found in the cave, a short walk downhill.

Uncovered from the late 19th century on, the natural cave intercepts a *wied*, or ravine, carved out of the hill by rushing torrents during the melting of an ice age. Caught in here were layers of detritus, including bones of wild animals. The human bones and carbonized grains found in the upper layers indicate that the cave was inhabited in Neolithic times and that the earliest settlers were an agricultural people. The cave is cool and restful, but there's not much to see except for stalactites and stalagmites.

Less than a mile away, on the way to St. George's Bay, is **Borġ in-Nadur,** a village that was fortified around 1500 B.C., with some remaining ruins and "cart-ruts" (see p. 14) nearby. Note the heavy wall fortifications.

Skorba at Żebbiegħ is the oldest dwelling site in Malta, with a wall built around 4000 B.C., remains of farmers' and herdsmens' huts and two megalithic temples.

Ħaġar Qim and Mnajdra can be reached via Żurrieq about 8 miles from Valletta. The site of **Ħaġar Qim** is spectacular—well above the sea, with a view onto Filfla island. Here you'll see a typical concave outer façade and a rather complex series of inside

Mystery pervades the Hypogeum, ancient cave-temple near Paola. Statue of "fat lady", opposite, may be clue to prehistoric fertility cult.

rooms. But the uniqueness of this temple lies in its construction material. It is almost wholly built of globigerina limestone, often pitted and weathered.

Interesting details here include various "mushroom" or "tea-table" altars in the second court as well as other altars with pit-hole decoration, a typical prehistoric Maltese temple decor. In the second "apse" on the right after entry, you'll see a small hole in a monolith and a space behind it, which may have been an oracle hole. One of Malta's famous "fat lady" figures was found in this temple. Known irreverently as "the Venus of Malta", the skirted cult-figure with piano legs but topless is now in the National Museum.

Mnajdra is a 5-minute walk down towards the sea on an even lovelier site. Contemporary with Ħaġar Qim, it is a complex of temples, with several features common to the former.

You reach the **Hal Saflieni Hypogeum** by going to PAOLA, a workers' suburb of Valletta. This eerie monument carved out of soft limestone is a vast, overwhelming, underground labyrinth, not recommended to sufferers from claustrophobia. Hypogeum is Greek for

"under-ground". The caves were hollowed out in areas on three different levels, descending to a depth of 40 feet, and were discovered by accident when workers were building houses and digging cisterns here in 1902. Professionally explored by archaeologist Sir Themistocles Zammit, it's one of Malta's most fascinating prehistoric sites.

You descend a modern spiral staircase into the ever-danker and growing gloom. The first level would seem to be the oldest and roughest-cut (around 3300 B.C.). The two lower levels were made around the time of the Ġgantija and Tarxien Temples (3200–2500 B.C.) and were carved out with increasing care and sophistication. The middle level has curved-in walls, corbelling, doors and niches resembling the features of the above-ground temples. This can be best appreciated in areas called the Main Chamber and Holy of Holies. Another spooky room is called the Oracle Chamber, with a hollow where men (only, it seems) can make an odd echo effect. In the Main Chamber was found the "sleeping lady" statuette (now in the National Museum). Some rooms have decoration in red or black in the form of spirals or hexagons; one "wall drawing" is supposed to be of a bull. One of the niches off this level has a 6-foot-deep hole and is called, ominously, "the snake pit".

Down a narrow staircase to the deepest part, you'll notice cubicles and pits for what look like very watery graves. The whole complex covers an area of 8,600 square feet and is estimated to have contained some 6,000 or 7,000 bodies. Sheltered from the weather, this is undoubtedly ancient Malta's best-preserved monument.

In contrast to the troglodytical Hypogeum, very much in the sun and a garden setting, the **Tarxien temple ruins,** only 400 yards away, make a cheery change. The temples here were discovered by a farmer who had trouble ploughing up his field with all these megalithic stones in them; then Sir Themistocles Zammit enthusiastically jumped at the chance to uncover a new site, which was done from 1915 to 1919.

The three temples were built at different times, but the high period dates from about 3200–2500 B.C.—the ultimate flowering of temple-building. First you'll see a museum with replicas of interesting carved stones found here, plus another piano-legged "fat lady". Then the first temple you come to contains replicas of lively bas-relief carvings—spirals, sheep, goats, pigs, cattle. Here you'll see yet another replica of a "fat lady", whose generous proportions will be an inspiration to weight-watchers.

The second temple is original in having six lobes or oval bays off the main corridor, instead of the usual four or five. Here you'll see a circular hearth, where the walls are rust-coloured from an ancient fire, possibly the result of the cremations. To the right is a small room containing slabs with interesting original carvings—bulls and a sow suckling her litter. Part of the floor has been removed to show the heavy stone balls that were used as rollers for the monolithic slabs.

The third temple of the group is the oldest including, a little further on, fragmented remains of the ancient Ġgantija-period temple. Beyond this, on the way out, you'll see a geometrically arranged series of round hollows in a big slab; this could have been a game, or used for divining purposes, though it's considered more likely that the depressions had to do with primitive libation ceremonies. **69**

Gozo

Called Calypso's Island, because the famed siren supposedly kept Ulysses enthralled there for seven blissful years, Gozo is still enchanting to people who like its sleepy pace and rustic whimsical charms. To the Maltese, it's known as Għawdex (pronounced "owdesh").

Gozo is Malta's small sister, only 9 miles long by 4½ miles wide, with a population of almost 30,000. And while its history and development parallel Malta's, Gozo has its own distinct characteristics. The natives, called Gozitans, are proud of their island.

Gozo is greener than Malta. The scenery is characterized by neat terraces and freestone fences, with big flat-topped mesas rising on the horizon, and bell-towers silhouetted against the sky of every town. The island is church-mad, and there are at least 29 parish churches, not to mention little chapels. A day in any town is punctuated throughout by church bells ringing their various messages.

While 20th-century traffic has taken over the small roads, life still goes on much as it did centuries ago. Gozo lives mainly on agriculture and fishing, with excellent crops of tomatoes, potatoes, melons, oranges and figs. People are close to the earth, and you'll still see farmers leading their flocks of goats or driving donkey carts, while little old ladies make lace in the shade of their doorways in the late afternoon.

Activity centres around the hub and capital city of Victoria, although there is much to see elsewhere. Many people try to cram Gozo into one day, but this is a shame, since the small island should be savoured at leisure. It not only has numerous interesting Baroque churches, but the spectacular Neolithic temples of Ġgantija, plus fascinating hikes and rough swimming. (Beach life can be beautiful here, but it's also primitive, and you won't find a sophisticated cabana setting.) There are few luxury hotels, but the small simple hotels and restaurants are delightful, and a growing number of farmhouses are being converted into holiday homes.

There is no airstrip on the island, so you go from Malta by ferry, private boat, or an excursion day tour from Sliema. Whichever route you take, from Sa Maison near Valletta or from Ċirkewwa, the short crossing is delightful. On the right, you'll pass uninhabited Cominetto rock and Comino with its watchtower, though you won't see the island's one hotel, in a bay on the other side. The name Comino comes from the herb cumin, which was once grown in abundance there.

The entry into Mġarr harbour is exciting, with several beautiful belfries looming up on the hills, the harbour itself alive with bobbing *luzzu* boats. On the left the tall steeple belongs to a 19th-century church, Our Lady of Lourdes. On the headland is Fort Chambray, built in the mid-18th century by a French knight. Later it became the prison, but since there wasn't much crime on Gozo, the prison closed (miscreants are sent to Malta) and the building is now to be converted into a tourist complex.

The ups and downs of Gozo's history are very similar to those of Malta's. From the prehistoric temples of Ġgantija, which have much in common with the Tarxien temples, to the aggression of the Turks, then British rule and finally independence, the story of Gozo reflects that of Malta.

GOZO

Victoria

The English doggedly call Gozo's bustling centre by the name given it during Queen Victoria's jubilee in 1897, though Gozitans call it by its old Arab name, Rabat. Just a short drive (about 3½ miles) from MĠARR, the town has a citadel situated on a bluff, which can be seen for miles.

The main street is **Republic Street** (Racecourse Street). On the left, Rundle Gardens are named after Sir Leslie Rundle, governor of Malta, 1909–15. During the August 15 Feast of the Assumption, this is the site of a charming little country fair. During the same period (and also on the Feast of St. George, third Sunday in July) a colourful horse and donkey race is run, when everybody turns out to see their friends race in sulkies or ride the mules bareback up Republic Street—quite a hilarious occasion.

It-Tokk is the attractive shady central square, with a war monument in the middle,

Spires of Our Lady of Lourdes church dominate Mġarr harbour, Gozo's gateway. Handmade pullovers (left) take hours of patient work.

edged with little shops, tiny tunnel-shaped bars and a bank. On one side is the 18th-century St. James' Church, on the other a rounded building that was built in 1733 to house the Banca Giuratala; today it is an information office though many local worthies seem to use the place as a haven for reading their newspapers.

During *festa* times, the square is a riot of colour with various religious statues; "Judas" is appropriately placed just outside the Inland Revenue Office, and there are garlands all over the square. But any morning it is a hub of seething activity with an open-air market. In the evenings, it swarms again, with people walking slowly up and down for the *passeggiata* or social hour.

Market times are good for exploring the back streets, when you'll see a lavish display of fish, fruit and vegetables, and hear lively banter between shoppers and sellers. The **old town** behind It-Tokk is very picturesque, with narrow alleyways and simple old houses.

On its own square, **St. George's Church** is a fine example of Baroque architecture, and very elaborately decorated. Though restored in the 19th and 20th centuries (with a whole new Romanesque-style roof), the original church was built much earlier, then improved and enlarged after 1673 when the Gozitans contributed their wealth and services in thanksgiving for having escaped a plague that raged that year. The most striking **painting** is by Mattia Preti over the choir altar, showing St. George with his foot victoriously poised on the dragon's head, his white charger by his side. The July festival is quite a bash, and there is a good deal of rivalry between St. George's and the cathedral, whose festival is the Assumption, August 15.

The citadel contains the **cathedral.** Behind the rather austere stone façade with its two huge bronze cannons at the entry is an elaborate interior. Built by Lorenzo Gafà between 1697 and 1711, it has an interesting and convincing *trompe l'œil* "dome" painted on a flat space by Antonio Manuele; the real dome was never finished. Be sure not to miss the coloured mosaic tombs of bishops and priests, with their family crests and Latin mottoes on the floor.

On the left as you enter is a rather histrionic statue of the Virgin, all in blue, her eyes and hands raised heavenward; this

20th-century work is carried all around town during the festival of the Assumption, and is posed on a very ornate and expensive-looking heavy silver pedestal.

The Cathedral Museum, at the back, houses collections of church ornaments, sacred vestments and paintings.

To the south of the Cathedral stands the Bondi Palace, containing the **Gozo National Museum.** The house, built around an inner courtyard, was once owned by a wealthy local family. Among the exhibits are amphorae from Roman times, a 12th-century tombstone of an Arab girl with a touching inscription, and shards and relics from various eras, especially the prehistoric phases. It has a model of Ġgantija as well as a large phallic symbol from one of Ggantija's temples. A visit will provide a good introduction to the temples you can see at Xagħra (see p. 79). Upstairs is a handsome headless female

VICTORIA (RABAT)

1 Cathedral
2 Gozo National Museum
3 St. Sabina
4 St. James'
5 St. George
6 Post Office
7 Bishop's Palace

THE CITADEL

ŻEBBUĠ

MARSALFORN

XEWKIJA, MĠARR

MĠARR, SANTA LUCIA

GĦARB

SANNAT, SANTA LUCIA

Milite Bernardo Cross Street

Cathedral Square

Castle Hill

Foreman Street

St Ursula's Street

Castle Street

Chedru St

Mgr. Luigi Vella Street

Sqaq Valley Street

Assumption Street

Republic Street (Racecourse Street)

St. Sabina Square

It-Tokk Sq.

De Soldanis Street

St. George's Square

St Mary's Street

St. George's Street

St. Market Street

St. Palm Street

Main Gate Street

School Street

Mgr. Farrugia Street

St. Andrew's St.

N

0   50   100   150 m
0   50   100   150 yards

XLENDI

MUNXAR, SANNAT, XEWKIJA

Roman statue, dated to the 1st century B.C.

Climb the steps on the other side of the cathedral courtyard and you'll reach the ramparts of the citadel. In a 20-minute walk around, you can admire marvellous **views** all over Gozo, with its flat-topped houses edging the meandering roads and a church on nearly every hilltop. The citadel and ramparts were strengthened after the brutal Turkish incursion and kidnappings of 1551. Dragut,

the North-African pirate (see p. 19), having failed in an assault against the knights in Malta, attacked the people of Gozo, carrying off between 6,000 and 7,000 islanders to slavery. Subsequently, Gozo was invaded many times by the Turks in the 16th century and gradually the stone dwellings of the citadel were abandoned. Though the rubble where goats graze looks as deserted as Ġgantija, it is earmarked for restoration with the assistance of UNESCO.

Worth the climb: from ramparts of Gozo's citadel at Victoria, you can look out over the entire isle.

Ġgantija Temples

To reach this ancient site, you take the road to Xagħra, but before entering town, on the right, there's a fenced enclosure. Here you'll find the most awe-inspiring of any temple group in the Maltese islands.

The Ġgantija temples were excavated at various times be-

tween 1827 and 1953. There are two of them, both facing south-east as most prehistoric temples in Malta do.

The older and bigger of the temples dates back to 3600–3300 B.C., a period sometimes referred to as the Copper Age (precursor to the Bronze Age), though there was no copper on Malta or Gozo then. Typical of this type of temple, the façade is slightly concave. The entry is flanked by two orthostats (upright stones), a big slab, and a concave stone where worshippers may have washed their feet. The left part of the façade is made of huge coralline limestone slabs, rising to a height of about 20 feet. Here you can really appreciate the name—Ġgantija—and legend says that a monstrous woman or a group of colossal giants built the temples.

The inside walls and decoration are of softer globigerina limestone. The lobe-shaped apses (five of them) contain a number of interesting features, including libation holes, an oracle hole (on the right) and stones carved with typical swirling patterns. In the second right-hand apse, you'll see a fireplace hole, probably used to keep an "eternal flame" burning.

One of the blocks on view **77**

once supported the huge phallic symbol in the Gozo National Museum. Two nearby apses and the rear apse constitute the "holy of holies", and were probably restricted to priests. This apse has impressively high walls—20 feet or so—and is curved inward, to make a semidome. The altar, with two holes, perhaps for draining animal blood, has three blocks with primitive pitting decorations, typical of the period.

The smaller temple is simpler and rather less interesting, with the rear or main apse and altar reduced to almost nothing. A walk outside around the walls shows the skill of these early builders, who used enormous blocks of hard coralline limestone, placed horizontally and vertically, some of them 16 feet long and weighing up to 50 tons. The technical feat performed by primitive men, who supposedly knew no mathematics, in erecting these blocks boggles the mind. It was hypothetically done by a system of levers and ramps, using both gravity and manpower in the manœuvring process. An excellent little booklet you can buy gives all the fine details.

A step through the doorway takes you into Gozo's past at Ġgantija.

Towns and Villages

North-west of Ġgantija, **Xagħra** was inhabited in prehistoric times. It's a pleasant town with an exuberantly decorated red "Baroque" 19th-century **church.** Signs point to Xerri's Cave and Ninu's Cave, and both are worth a short visit. Guides will point out the amusing shapes of the stalactites and stalagmites.

At the north-east corner of the Xagħra plateau, with a superb view over to Ramla Bay on the right, you come to **Calypso's Cave,** where Ulysses supposedly dallied with the siren. One wonders what either Calypso or Ulysses saw in this place, as the narrow staircase leads to a singularly unimpressive and murky hole.

Almost directly across the central road to Mġarr, is **Xewkija,** a rather plain town with an awesome **church,** started in 1952 and only finished after 30 years' labour. Built to a classical design in golden globigerina limestone, it is a typical Gozitan accomplishment, realized by the labour and devotion of the town's 3,500 citizens. The **dome** here is even bigger than Malta's Mosta, and the third or fourth largest in the world. (Internal diameter 80 ft., height 245 ft.). The parishioners wanted the church so badly, they built it right over the old one, only removing the first when the new building could be used.

Xlendi is reached by a small road leading south-west out of Victoria. Two miles from the island capital, it is a lovely natural site worth the trip, though it can be crowded. On the way, you'll see hilly pastoral scenery, a monumental wash-house on the left adorned with the arms of the Order, and, at a turning on the right, the slaughter-house. Xlendi is beautifully situated at the end of a long *wied* (a natural fissure in the rock caused by erosion).

The pastel houses of the town are tucked away at the end of a long narrow bay surrounded by two high rocky promontories. (Along the left-hand promontory is a favourite place for swimming, and the right-hand one, with its natural rock garden and wild flowers, is a popular place for walkers.) With hotels, cafés and restaurants, Xlendi is a favourite excursion haunt. Tourists love the little shops where lace, woven goods and other local specialities are sold.

An adjacent road out of Victoria leads to **Sannat,** a tiny town reputed for its lace-making. Just outside is the island's only luxury hotel, Ta'Ċenċ, built in native stone and discreetly hidden in the countryside. It's near a huge new reservoir that is a boon to the neighbouring towns. Ta'Ċenċ is also in the vicinity of a site full of prehistoric "cart tracks" (see p. 14).

All roads lead from Victoria, and Marsalforn is about $2\frac{1}{2}$ miles to the north-east. On the way, you'll see several windmills and, to the left, a statue of Christ crowning a peak.

Once a quiet old fishing

A lovely place to soak up the sun—Xlendi village.

town, **Marsalforn** has become a popular bathing place, especially the over-crowded spit of sand, but equally the rock ledges.

From Marsalforn, a road leads through some rugged country a couple of miles up to ZEBBUĠ, which has little of merit except good views. (You can also take a larger road from Victoria.) There is a quaint informal exhibit here which a local family would be glad to show you. Ask anybody for the house of Sebastian Axiak, a local farmer who turned his hand to sculpting and made a big **diorama;** he died years ago, but the family is happy to display the diorama, a charming potpourri of Christian lore, village scenes and bell-towers from all over the world.

West of Victoria is Gozo's most primitive and, some think, prettiest area. Latest of all places to have been settled, it was once called "the desert".

On a side road between GĦAMMAR and Għarb is a curious church, **Ta'Pinu,** built between 1920 and 1936. This incongruous neo-Romanesque affair is surrounded with oleanders and a circle of large white statues depicting the Stations of the Cross, but its main interest lies in the miracles connected with it. This was the site of a rather run-down chapel (1534), which had been cared for by a pious man named Gauci, nicknamed Pinu. On June 22, 1883, a peasant woman named Carmela Grima heard a mysterious voice urging her to say three *aves.* She heard a similar voice several times, and a friend of hers, Francesco Portelli, admitted he had heard voices too. The two prayed for his desperately ill mother, who recovered miraculously, and from then on miracles multiplied. Ta'Pinu is still a famous shrine and place of pilgrimage.

Nearby, just outside Għarb, the museum is a quaint little place with small objects and dioramas made by the pious Portelli and Carmela Grima. To see the museum, ask the parish priest at Ta'Pinu, who can arrange to have it opened.

Għarb is the perfect little Gozitan village boasting a lovely Baroque church on its main square. With pastel house-fronts, a tiny village shop and little to do except watch the women making lace, the scene is so peaceful that it almost seems unreal. The square is beautifully decorated with coloured pillars and lights at *festa* time in early July.

Back towards Victoria, take

a small road outside Gharb through SAN LAWRENZ, then left about a mile down to **Dwejra** for some spectacular sightseeing and bathing. Across the cliffs as you descend is a big outcrop in the water—Fungus Rock, so named for a fungus growing there which was once prized by the knights for its curative haemostatic powers. The bay below is dominated by Qawra Tower, built in 1651. Just beyond, a little chapel to the left is on an extraordinary rock promontory with a natural opening. Down a rocky road to the right is the **Inland Sea,** a quiet salt-water pool with a scenic tunnel through which you can swim (about 10–15 minutes) or ride in a fisherman's boat out to the open sea. There are no amenities here, but a friendly fisherman's hut opens up as a "bar" in the summer.

Nadur, 3½ miles east of Victoria, is the second largest town in Gozo, population 4,300, and the richest. The people are proud of their parish **church,** built by G. Bonnici in the 18th century, restored in the 19th, and rich in elaborate and expensive decor. The town is at quite an altitude for Gozo—500 feet above sea-level—and the name Nadur means "summit" in Arabic.

For isolated rock bathing in a very pretty and spectacular setting, you can take a little rutty road north of Nadur, then walk down past the orange groves to **San Blas.** Another road leads 2 miles to **Ramla Bay,** where you'll find Gozo's big golden-sand beach. It has a simple bar in summer, and plenty of sunning space despite its popularity. North of Ramla is GHAJN BARRANI, accessible only by a primitive road which stops at the head of a cliff that you have to scramble down; but the setting is lovely, and the rocks are flat—for sunbathing or picnics.

QALA is a simple country town whose windmill is the last one working in Gozo. Further on are coves with good bathing, and quarries whose main claim to fame is that they supplied the white stone for the new Roman Catholic Cathedral of Liverpool.

As in Malta, almost everything is an excursion on Gozo. If you're staying there, a pleasant half-day's outing can be made by hiring a boat for a trip around GOZO and COMINO. There are lovely rocky outcrops and headlands, and you can stop in the popular blue lagoon for a refreshing swim in limpid turquoise water.

What to Do

Sports

With its beneficent climate, Malta is a paradise for all outdoor sports most of the year. About the only things you can't do here are ski and ice skate. Naturally, water sports come first on the islands, but hiking around the rocky headlands and to archaeological sites can be a wonderful—and free—occupation in the cooler months.

Swimming

It's free everywhere except for a few spots where you can rent a mat or chaise-longue for a reasonable price and enjoy the benefits of a bar or restaurant. There are about a dozen small sandy beaches on Malta, less on Gozo. Best bets in Malta are Golden Bay, Għajn Tuffieħa, Ġnejna Bay, Paradise Bay and Mellieħa Bay. On Gozo, the big sandy crescent is Ramla Bay. San Blas Bay is smaller and less accessible.

But even prettier scenery and snorkelling can be enjoyed at the rocky beach sites (and you won't get sand in your sandwiches). Some of these are Peter's Pool and Għar Lapsi

Pool; St. Paul's Bay; Marsaskala. Sliema offers flat rocks for sunbathing, but sometimes the area is crowded. Gozo's attractive rock-bathing beaches include Xlendi (some sand as well), the Inland Sea (Dwejra), Marsalforn, Mġarr ix-Xini, Daħlet Qorrot, and Qala (near the desalination plant).

Water Skiing

The larger beaches and big hotels offer most water sports and facilities. There's water skiing at St. Paul's Bay, Mellieħa, Sliema, Salina Bay, St. George's Bay, Golden Bay.

Windsurfing (Board Sailing)

Windsurfing has become common in Malta, particularly in the sheltered bays of the north (Ramla, Mellieħa, St. Paul's, St. George's, Marsaskala).

Scuba Diving and Snorkelling

Snorkelling is good everywhere you swim, and is a sport you can do with minimal instruction. Masks and breathing equipment may be bought, or you can rent everything at beach centres, including flippers and safety floats.

Scuba diving and instruction are available at St. Julian's, St. Paul's Bay and Mellieħa Bay. You must hold a diving permit, available from local health authorities. The scuba diving centres will give you full instruction. You can also go on diving trips to Gozo and Comino.

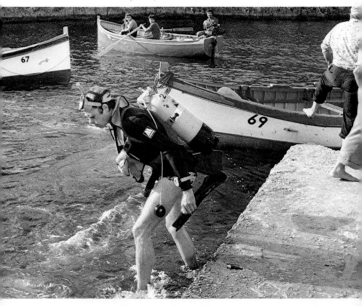

Boating and Sailing

As a top Mediterranean seaport, Malta naturally has excellent facilities, and if you don't come in your own boat, you can rent anything from a luxury craft right down to a simple dinghy. Information on berthing, repairs, and firms chartering boats is available from Malta Yachting Centre, Manoel Island Bridge, Gżira. See p. 105 for rental charges. The Valletta Yacht Club on Manoel Island accepts temporary members.

Fishing

It's free and you don't need a licence. If you want to go out early with a fisherman, inquire informally around Marsaxlokk Bay or in Mġarr harbour on Gozo. A fisherman might take you out for a small fee or even for nothing.

Sea swimming and sailing are two of many outdoor sports in Malta.

The Marsa Sports Club

This sports centre is the main place to offer many inland sports, including golf, tennis, squash, riding, cricket—and billiards. It is $2^{1}/_{2}$ miles south of Valletta at Marsa, on the way to Luqa Airport, and has a modern, fully equipped club house with a bar and restaurant. The club has over a dozen hard tennis courts, an 18-hole golf-course and a squash court. Riding, polo and horse-racing can also be found at Marsa.

Spectator Sports

The Maltese are mad about **football** (soccer). Main matches of the Malta Football Association take place at the national stadium at Ta'Qali (Mdina) from October to June. Another sports stadium is at Marsa.

Water-polo is played all over the island, under the aegis of the Amateur Swimming Association. Inquire at the Tourist Organization.

Other Sports

There is a big bowling centre at Msida (Enrico Mizzi Street), open daily from 10 a.m. to 1 a.m. Archery, table tennis and badminton are also available through the Marsa Sports Club.

Shopping

There are a few department stores on Malta, but you'll probably make most of your purchases in small specialized shops or buy from outdoor stalls. Prices are reasonable on the whole, and the figure shown or quoted is the real price; haggling is not a way of life here. For shopping hours, see HOURS, p. 117.

Best Buys

Malta and Gozo are a bonanza if you're in the market for silver, glass, ceramics, cotton goods, sturdy woollen knits, woven gloves and lace. Ta'Qali just outside Mdina, is a place you want ' to try, a crafts village that welcomes visitors. Here, in "quonset huts" on a converted airstrip, you can see artisans at work and buy their wares inexpensively. The glass factory offers lovely shapes and marbled colours in hand-blown Mdina glass. The subtle blend of turquoise blue and bottle green is outstanding, as is another combination of browns. This unique look was started by two Englishmen and enthusiastically adopted by the Maltese. You'll see everything here from vaguely triangular decorative fish to goblets and "Ming" jars.

The silver and filigree shown at Ta'Qali is interesting, including many Maltese crosses, rings, bracelets of varied design, cigarette boxes and candelabra.

The pottery and ceramics are rather rustic but of high quality, including brown and blue fired vases, ash trays, dishes of all sizes, and other objects that could not fail to look pretty in a country setting. A workshop also sells "Malta Stone", a type of banded calcite worked into bookends, ash trays and so on.

There is also a crafts centre opposite the cathedral in St. John's Square, Valletta, and other shops selling the same type of goods described above, especially dazzling silver. Maltese silver is reputed to have the highest pure silver content in the world. Gold can also be a good buy in Malta—small objects and jewellery.

Weaving, knitting and lace-making are still flourishing on Gozo (sometimes sold on Malta), and Gozo's main good buys are lace and woollen knits. The lace can be very delicate, on handkerchiefs, all-lace doilies, or as edging for place-

Life in the Mediterranean is lived outdoors, even the shopping—for seafood or clothing or souvenirs.

mats, napkins and tablecloths, attractive in oatmeal-coloured linen. Triangular loosely knit shawls are inexpensive and useful for cool evenings. And you might want to take home a Gozo sweater—either a practical, nautical-looking pullover or a belted cardigan with a shawl collar, usually in white or off-white, sometimes in subtle colours as well. The wool varies from very soft, almost angora quality to rather prickly. Best places to shop on Gozo are around Victoria's It-Tokk square, in Xlendi and Marsalforn, and in the crafts village of Ta'Dbiegi at San Lawrenz.

Other good buys on both Malta and Gozo include inexpensive cotton goods: bikini bathing costumes, nice dish towels, funny bikini underwear for women, attractive T-shirts for women and men, and jeans (Gozo makes them).

Naturally, you'll find plenty of colourful postcards and the run-of-the-mill "scene" souvenirs—ash trays, flags and so on with *luzzu* or *dghajsa* boats, knights' fortifications and watchtowers, the Maltese Cross and knights' coats of arms all over the place. Wrought ironware is becoming an interesting local buy, and traditional brass dolphin door-knockers make good souvenirs.

90

Festivals

The Maltese are a very festive people, celebrating anything at the drop of a hat; luckily there are dozens of religious holidays throughout the year. Unique to the Maltese islands are the saint days, celebrated as joyous *festi*. Every parish (64 in Malta and 14 in Gozo) celebrates its patron saint day, though dates vary and are usually on the weekend after the day itself.

Most **festi** happen throughout the summer, beginning with three days of prayer services preceding the eve of the celebration. Thanksgiving mas-

National Tourist Organization - Malta

ses are said in the mornings, and the churches are decorated with flowers, huge silver candlesticks, and sometimes red silk damask hangings. Outside, the façades are lit by garlands of light. On the eve of the feastday the main religious service is marked by the removal of the holy relic from the side chapel to the altar. On the day itself, brass bands parade around town, while groups of men carry a statue of the saint, and the joyous crowd has a ball with fireworks and ice-cream cones. There is a concert in the town's main square, followed by an often excellent fireworks display, usually on Saturday night. The Tourist Office can supply you with the dates.

Christmas and Easter are celebrated solemnly but also with good food (the *figolla* is a traditional Easter sweet), gaiety and goodwill. Good Friday is marked by processions with marching, hooded *penitentes* carrying statues in the streets, as in Spain or South America.

National Day falls on March 31. It is celebrated at Valletta and Vittoriosa with

Fanciful costumes, dancing and merriment enliven the Maltese carnival.

parades, marching bands, fireworks and sporting events.

Carnival is quite a lively occasion in Malta, held before Lent, generally falling in late February. The celebrations begin with the dancing of the *parata,* a sword dance, to commemorate the knights' victory over the Turks in the siege of 1565. The high point of carnival was in the 18th century, when the knights paraded in grand carriages, to the accompaniment of drums and fireworks.

The **Imnarja** is a folk festival held on the Feast of St. Peter and St. Paul (June 29th) in Buskett Gardens, with lots of music, singing and dancing, plus horse and donkey races nearby.

On September 8, the feast day for Our Lady of Victories, the celebrations of victory in the two Great Sieges include the **Regatta** in Grand Harbour. Muscular oarsmen battle for prizes and honour amid a bedlam of sirens, horns and cheers. The sailors' turn comes in the **Autumn Races** organized by the Valletta Yacht Club one week in October.

Republic Day on December 13 is marked by a public holiday and parades, music and fireworks, particularly in Vittoriosa.

Nightlife

Nightlife is mainly limited to the resort areas—Sliema, St. Julian's, Buġibba/Qawra—where there's plenty of activity. It's mostly quite informal, centred around the handful of discos and the bars and pubs which put on entertainment. And it doesn't go on very late.

Theatre and Concerts

At the Manoel Theatre in Valletta, you can see ballet performances or hear concerts by the Manoel Symphony Orchestra and international soloists and groups throughout most of the year except for the hottest summer months. There are amateur dramatic societies that put on occasional plays in the theatre, and in the summer there are sometimes Shakespeare performances outdoors at San Anton Gardens. You can get details of current productions from *What's On.*

Gozo has two big, elaborately decorated theatres, and there are a few plays and operas running throughout the winter.

Cinema

There are a number of cinemas in Valletta and Sliema, and the odd one in certain villages. Films are mostly shown in English, a few in Italian.

Gozo has only a few cinemas, in Victoria, but each shows a different film every day through most of the year, except in July and August.

Dancing

There are no real floor-show nightclubs in Malta or Gozo, but some of the big hotels have live music for dinner dancing. A few restaurants offer barbecues, music and folklore dancing. There are various "Malta by Night" tours, folklore evenings, "Medieval Banquets" and similar evening excursions and entertainments.

Discotheque life is as lively as anywhere else, especially among the young. There are several discotheques around Malta, especially in Sliema and St. Julian's, and a few lively ones on Gozo. Some are even partially or totally outdoors, which is magnificent in the summer. Unfortunately for night crawlers, but fortunately for local inhabitants, discos close down at midnight to curb "noise pollution", though some clubs stay open later. All disco clubs are accessible to anybody with the money to pay.

Casino

Malta's modern casino, at Dragonara Point, St. George's Bay, attracts many fanatic or casual gamblers. You're advised to bring your passport (no Maltese citizens are allowed entry) when you play here—and only as much money as you're prepared to lose. The casino opens at 8 p.m. and closes well after midnight, depending on the action.

Dining Out in Malta

The *best* of Maltese food is rich with hearty Mediterranean flavour and colour—juicy red tomatoes, gleaming onions, dark or light green peppers, tender squash or marrow, the freshest of fish, often with exotic names. Garlic, olive oil and herbs play an important part too, although the British with roasts or fish and chips and Italians with pasta and sauces have undoubtedly been the big influences. Maltese cooking does exist, and if you keep your eyes open, you'll spot a few authentic Maltese specialities on the menu.

Both Malta and Gozo have made an effort in the restaurant field, and you can eat well for a reasonable price, especially simple things like fresh *fettucini* or grilled swordfish with lemon. The Maltese bread—with a crisp brown crust and soft inside—is a real treat. On the other hand, what passes as "French" bread is a bland and rather tasteless roll.

As for the type of restaurants you choose, you'll find everything from the simple, neon-lit place (where you can usually eat for next to nothing) up to a vast outdoor garden or seaside terrace with candlelight at night and attentive service. Restaurants are classified into four grades by the government with the price ranging accordingly. Hours of serving are roughly the same as on the Continent: lunch 12 noon to 2 or 2.30 p.m. and dinner 7 to 10 p.m.

Breakfasts may be Continental or English-style (sausage, eggs and bacon).

Antipasti

You'll often see starters or hors d'oeuvres listed the Italian way. These may include slices of local pepper sausages, Parma ham *(prosciutto)* and melon, black or green olives, mixed little vegetable platters (as in Italy), shrimp cocktail or smoked salmon.

Soup and Pasta

The most frequent soup on the menu is *minestra*, a hearty vegetable concoction that is thicker than the Italian version *(minestrone)*, and made with just about everything in the kitchen garden: onion, potato, broad or haricot beans, cabbage, zucchini (baby marrow), pumpkin, tomatoes or tomato puree, and some pasta. It's a meal in itself! If you see fish soup, try it, especially if you like a highly seasoned flavour.

Fresh tomato soup is excellent, and menus often offer good consommé.

All kinds of pasta are popular with the Maltese, and very good. *Timpana*, if you can get it (usually only in a Maltese home), is a true Maltese dish to make you forget any diet: flaky pastry filled with macaroni, minced meat, onions, tomato puree, aubergines (eggplant), eggs and cheese, unmoulded and served in slices. A simpler version sometimes seen in small cafés is macaroni moulded with egg and cheese.

If you like Italian food, you can do almost as well as in Naples. Many restaurants have nearly all-Italian menus, so you can take along your Italian phrase book. Otherwise, menus usually appear in English, with occasionally a few French dishes listed in French.

You'll see all versions of Italian pasta, like *tortellini al sugo Bolognese* (little meat-filled pasta preparations with tomato-meat sauce), *tagliatelle alla crema* (flat noodles with cream), *vermicelli alle vongole* (tiny vermicelli with clams). Maltese *ravjul* is a tasty version of ricotta-stuffed ravioli. Many restaurants offer delicious *risotto* dishes, based on rice and cooked with various vegetables and sea-food.

Fish and Shellfish

Fish is top fare in Malta and it's treated with respect, which means flavour is enhanced, rather than being disguised with exotic sauces. *Lampuka* is Malta's "own" fish, and the season, beginning in late August and going through to November, is a big moment. The first day of *lampuki*-running, the fishermen raise their little triangular flags in salute. It is a firm-fleshed white fish, and may be served grilled, casseroled with wine and herbs, with piquant sauce, or in a kind of pie *(torta tal-lampuki)*, or pre-fried and cooked in a pastry shell with onion, tomatoes, cauliflower, spinach and perhaps olive oil and walnuts.

Octopus, squid *(calamari)* and cuttlefish are often eaten cold in salad, as a stew with curry flavour, or stuffed.

Fresh fish dishes usually include grilled swordfish, fried or grilled red mullet or *merluzzo*, tunny (tuna), *dentici* (dentex) or *ćerna* (grouper). Grouper may also be steamed whole and served in butter or in a piquant sauce. Any fish *alla Maltese* means served with a tomato and green pepper sauce. Fried scampi (prawns) are popular, and, as in most places in the world, lobster is prized and expensive. **95**

Meat

Most restaurants offer international specialities, perhaps something like *filet de bœuf sauce béarnaise* (fillet of beef with *béarnaise* sauce); but watch for something typically Maltese such as *braġoli* or beef olives. These are a type of beef *paupiette* or roll stuffed with bacon, breadcrumbs, hard-boiled egg, parsley and a touch of garlic, fried, then simmered with onions and wine.

Beef or lamb dishes in Maltese homes are usually a kind of casserole in which the meat has been cooked with potatoes and onions. This is what roast beef "Maltese-style" means if you see it on the menu. Most island meat specialities don't appear on menus—things like braised pork, ox-tongue in a wine sauce or fricassee of meat balls with sweetbread or brains.

You'll often see good beef and veal on menus, Italian-style. *Filetto alla Meranese*, for example, is beef fillet wrapped in bacon and served in good brown sauce. *Vitello alla Marsala* would be veal scaloppini with Marsala wine sauce; veal

A refreshing breeze adds to the pleasure of dining out in Malta.

may also be breaded and deep-fried.

Leg of lamb or lamb chops are popular, and sometimes lamb is served shish kebab-style, on skewers.

The pork produced on Malta was renowned for its texture and flavour, but in 1979 a disease struck Maltese pigs, and they all had to be destroyed. Now new, uncontaminated pigs are being raised on Comino, and pork is back in circulation again.

Fenek (coniglio in Italian) means rabbit, and is a favourite sometimes served in restaurants—fried, stewed or casseroled with wine and garlic, curried, or as a delicious tart *(torta tal-fenek)* with pork, peas, tomatoes and spice.

When you're served country-raised chicken, you're in for a treat; it may be roasted, *alla diavola* or *diable* (grilled with shallot, mustard, breadcrumbs) or perhaps even *à la Kiev*—breast with a melting butter-herb filling that serves as the sauce.

Vegetables

There are always good, fresh vegetables available, no matter how bad the drought. The potatoes are delicious, whether sautéed, baked or as chips (French fries). Baby new potatoes in butter are a special treat. You'll have excellent mixed salads, perhaps creamed spinach or buttered beans *(fagioli)*. And sometimes you can sample fried or ricotta-stuffed aubergines (eggplant) and baby marrow (zucchini) as well as stuffed tomatoes or green peppers.

Cheese and Dessert

Many restaurants serve excellent Italian cheese—Parmesan, Ricotta, Gorgonzola, Bel Paese —plus other imports like Gruyère, Cheddar and sometimes Roquefort. You might see the dry Maltese ewe cheese, deliciously spiked with peppercorns; another type, found in country towns, is aged in brine and capers. Perhaps the most common local sheep's milk cheese is called *ġbejna.*

An ideal dessert is fruit: fresh figs, plums and peaches are juicy-sweet and abundant in summer. Tangerines and oranges are wonderful in the winter, and at various periods strawberries, melons and mulberries are available. The prickly pear is intriguing, but its seeds can be a nuisance.

The Maltese have a sweet tooth, so there's plenty of Italian-style, creamy ice-cream available everywhere in many flavours. Some sweet-shops and restaurants sell fancy *semifreddo* or semi-cold ice-cream-cake confections.

Restaurants usually serve some type of *gâteau* or *torta* (cakes made with chocolate, almonds, fruits and so on) and fruit tarts. Ricotta is sometimes used in sweet cheesecakes with fruit or combined with chocolate, cherries, sugar and almonds to fill little cornets called *kannoli tar-rikotta*.

Festivals bring their own sweets too. At Eastertime, you'll see *figolli* in the shops, delicious iced almond-lemon biscuits (cookies) cut in various shapes—men, women, or baskets. Shops display all kinds of iced cakes at all times of year, but especially flavoursome are sesame rings, macaroons and treacle rings. A favourite confection at carnival time is *prinjolata*, a mouth-watering combination of sponge fingers, butter cream and almonds or pine nuts, decorated with chocolate and cherries. During all *festi*, you'll see stands selling almond nougat and other sweets.

Snacks
Many little bars sell lunch or snack food—simple things like meat-filled pasties. *Pastizzi* is a Maltese speciality: a flaky puff-pastry turnover with a filling of ricotta, pea-and-onion or anchovy. You can also get various sandwiches: chicken, ham-and-cheese and so on.

If you make sandwiches for your picnic, do as the Maltese do: pack big pieces of the local bread or rolls with olives, tomato, onion, anchovies, hard-boiled egg, tuna and whatever else you can squeeze in, plus a generous sprinkling of olive oil.

Drinks and Wine
The fruit juices are excellent, especially fresh, but also the cartons you see everywhere. Try the peach, apricot, pear and exotic mixtures. Coffee, tea and all types of soft drink are readily available. *Kinnie* is the local non-alcoholic thirst-quencher, though its odd sweet taste does not appeal to all visitors. The usual alcoholic drinks are served almost everywhere, with gin-and-tonic or Scotch the perennial British favourites. Many types of beer are sold. The local lager, *Farson's Cisk* ("chisk") is good, and inexpensive.

No one claims the wine is world class, but it's tasty—and heady.

at first, they have a fairly high alcoholic content. Reds tend to be rather heavy and sometimes a bit sharp, and are best drunk slightly chilled. These include *Marsovin Special Reserve*, *Lachryma Vitis*, *La Valette* (considered the best), *Farmers* and *Festa*.

White wines, nicely balanced between dry and fruity qualities and drunk well-chilled, are quite refreshing. Brands sold are *Lachryma Vitis*, *Marsovin Special Reserve*, *Marsovin*

Sauterne (very sweet, this one), *Farmers* and *Festa*. Beware of the mild to drastic laxative effect a large quantity of these wines can produce in the uninitiated.

Gozo produces fairly respectable wine, including *Velson's* red and white. The *Ġgantija* wines (red and white) are sweet, high in alcohol content, and have been known to produce excitable behaviour when drunk in quantity by non-Gozitans.

Read the Menu

The list below contains a selection of the words (Maltese, Italian and French) that you might come across on a Maltese menu.

abbachio, agnello, agneau	lamb
aċċola	amberjack (a fish)
aglio, ail	garlic
anitra, canard	duck
antipasto	starter (appetizer), hors d'œuvre
asparagi, asperges	asparagus
bistecca (alla boscaiola)	beefsteak (with wine-mushroom sauce)
boeuf, manzo	beef
braġoli, bragioli	beef olive *(paupiettes)*
brodu	clear consommé
calamari	squid
carciofi, qaqoċċ	artichoke
ċerna	grouper fish *(mérou)*
coniglio, lapin, fenek	rabbit
costata, costicine	chop, little chop
dentiċi, dentice	dentex (a fish)

dolce	sweet, dessert
espadon, pesce spada	swordfish
fagioli, fagiolini, haricots	beans
formaggio, fromage	cheese
frutta	fruit
funghi, champignons	mushrooms
gâteau	cake
ġbejna	Maltese sheep's milk cheese
homard, astice	lobster
insalata, salade	salad
lampuka	type of dolphin-fish special to Malta
melanzana	aubergine, eggplant
melone	melon
minestra	minestrone, thick vegetable soup
naranja	orange
pastizzi	turnover pastry with stuffing
patate, pommes de terre	potatoes
pesce, poisson	fish
piselli, petits pois	peas
prinjolata	special rich Maltese cake (for festivals)
prosciutto, jambon (e melone/ fichi) (avec melon/figues)	ham (with melon/figs)
riso, riz	rice
risotto (pescatora)	rice dish with other ingredients (with shellfish)
saltimbocca	veal scallops with ham and herbs
salsa	sauce
scaloppini, escalope de veau	veal scallop
scampi, crevette	shrimp, prawn
tagliatelli, pâtes	flat noodles
timpana	Maltese speciality of meat and cheese in a pastry case
torta	cake
tortellini	small, stuffed pasta
tonn, tonno, thon	tunny (tuna)
uove, œufs	eggs
vitello, veau	veal
vongole	clams
zuppa, soppa, soupe	soup
zucchini, qarabali, courgettes	baby marrows

BLUEPRINT for a Perfect Trip

How to Get There

Considering the wide choice of ways to go and the complexity of fares and regulations, you'd be well advised to put yourself into the hands of a reliable travel agent. It's the best way of meeting your timetable and your budget.

BY AIR

Malta's Luqa airport (see also p. 106) is on several European and some North-African routes. Travellers from other parts of the world will normally have to fly to a European capital (e.g. Rome, Frankfurt or London) for connecting flights to Malta.

Ask about discounts for children, youths, students and senior citizens, as well as special fares, including excursion and night tickets.

BY RAIL, ROAD AND SEA

Provided you have plenty of time and plan your journey carefully, the trip by **train** can be enjoyable. Travellers from northern Europe will have to change trains at least once, either in Milan or Rome. Be sure to make advance reservations for sleeping car or couchette.

Discounted train fares are available to senior citizens, youths, children and groups. Any travel agency can give you details of special deals.

If you're taking your **car** south to Malta, you can travel right across the Continent by motorway (expressway). You'll have to pay a toll on motorway routes through France, Switzerland and Italy, as well as for the tunnels through the Alps.

Taking the **car-train** adds to the cost of the journey, but many drivers feel the saving in wear and tear is well worth the extra expense.

The best **ferry** connections to Malta are from Naples, Reggio di Calabria, and Catania and Syracuse in Sicily. Ships from all these ports carry both passengers and cars. In addition, a fast catamaran carries passengers only between Malta and several Sicilian ports.

When to Go

Malta has a typical Mediterranean climate, with hot, dry summers and mild, humid winters. Even in winter you can expect a few hours of sunshine most days. Mediterranean waters stay warm the year round, making swimming possible from May to November. In May and from about mid-September to mid-October, the sirocco blows in from Africa, raising the humidity. Sea breezes moderate the heat of summer.

Trees and plants flower early on the island; spring blossoms are at their peak here in mid-March. After that, the temperature climbs rapidly, and the landscape takes on its characteristic parched appearance. Summer is the main tourist season in Malta, but increasing numbers of people are taking advantage of lower winter prices to enjoy a break from cold northern Europe.

		J	F	M	A	M	J	J	A	S	O	N	D
Air temperature													
Average daily	°F	58	59	61	65	71	79	84	85	81	75	67	61
maximum*	°C	14	15	16	18	22	26	29	29	27	24	20	16
Average daily	°F	50	51	52	56	61	67	72	73	71	66	60	54
minimum*	°C	10	10	11	13	16	19	22	23	22	19	16	12
Water temperature													
	°F	58	58	58	59	64	70	75	78	77	74	67	61
	°C	14	14	14	15	18	21	24	26	25	23	19	16

*Maximum temperatures are measured in the early afternoon, minimum temperatures just before sunrise.

Planning Your Budget

To give you an idea of what to expect, here is a list of average prices in Malta Liri (Lm). They can only be approximate, especially where competing prices prevail (e.g. car hire, souvenirs, water sports).

Airport transfer. Taxi to Valletta, official fare Lm 5.

Baby-sitters. Lm 1–1.50 per hour.

Car hire. Officially, the daily tariff is Lm 7 irrespective of make of car but exclusive of petrol. Garage rates in general and last-minute bookings in summer tend to exceed this level; out-of-season rates and advance reservations made before arrival can be less.

Cigarettes. Maltese brands 20–50¢ per packet of 20.

Ferry to Gozo. From Ċirkewwa to Mġarr, return, adults Lm 1.50, children 75¢, Lm 3.50 per car. From Sa Maison Pier, Pietà, fares are slightly higher.

Food and drinks. Set meal (tourist menu) in medium-priced restaurant Lm 2–3, bottle of local wine from 55¢, soft drinks 20¢, coffee 25¢.

Guides. Up to 12 people: 4 hours Lm 6, 8 hours Lm 9. Both rates must be topped with a free lunch for the guide or Lm 2 as compensation for lunch.

Hairdressers. *Woman's* shampoo and set Lm 2.50–3.50, haircut, shampoo and blow-dry Lm 3–3.95. *Man's* haircut from Lm 1.50, cut and blow-dry from Lm 2.50.

Hotels (single room with breakfast). ***** Lm 25–36, **** Lm 17.50–24, *** Lm 6–10, ** Lm 5.60–8, * Lm 4–6. Aparthotels and similar: Lm 5–10, depending on quality and facilities. Guest houses: Lm 4–6.

Shopping bag. Beef, fresh from Lm 3 per kilo, frozen from Lm 1.20 per kilo, chicken (frozen) Lm 1 per kilo; potatoes 15¢ per kilo; loaf of bread 13¢ for 750 grams; butter 20¢ for 227 grams; milk 12 ¢ per bottle; local wine 22–90¢ per bottle, whisky/gin Lm 5 per bottle.

Souvenirs. Set of three Maltese lace mats Lm 2.95–6.50, silver cuff links with Maltese cross Lm 5–6, gold filigree brooch Lm 24, silver filigree brooch Lm 3–8.

Water sports. *Rowing boat* Lm 1.50–2 per hour, *sailing dinghy* Lm 5–10 per person for two hours, *windsurfer* Lm 3 per hour, *water skiing* Lm 5 for 15 minutes' lesson, *scuba diving* (boat dives) Lm 7 per dive.

An A–Z Summary of Practical Information and Facts

> A star (*) following an entry indicates that relevant prices are to be found on page 105.

A **AIRPORT*.** The Maltese islands are served by Luqa airport, some 6 kilometres south of Valletta, a driving time of about 15 minutes. The airport accommodates jumbo jets, and is used by Air Malta and some other international airlines. Customs formalities are fairly simple, with the usual red and green channels. There's a currency-exchange counter open 24 hours a day. The airport has an air-conditioned restaurant, a snack bar, bookstall and car hire desks. The small duty-free shop sells tobacco, perfume, wines and spirits—you can also buy on arrival. An Air Malta information counter helps with inquiries and problems. The airport post office is open Monday to Saturday from 7 a.m. to 7 p.m.

The bus stop for Valletta is a two-minute walk from the terminal building. Some hotels run an airport minibus service; alternatively, taxis are available.

There's no airport on Gozo, though there is a helicopter link in summer; see "Ferries" under TRANSPORT for how to get there.

Note: Summer travellers are advised to reach the airport well in advance of the return flight. It is not unknown for certain airlines to overbook and "bump" passengers at the last minute.

Flight inquiries: tel. 622915
622876

B **BICYCLE HIRE.** Cycling can be strenuous (particularly under the Maltese summer sun), but the islands' flat terrain and reasonable dimensions lend themselves admirably to the sport. Cycles can be rented for relatively little; in this way, you avoid traffic jams, parking problems and general harassment. For further details, consult the Tourist **106** Organization (see TOURIST INFORMATION OFFICES).

CAMPING. There are no organized campsites on Malta and Gozo.

CAR HIRE*. See also DRIVING. Major international car hire firms operate in Malta, as do dozens of small free-lance agencies, some reliable, others less so. In any case, rental terms are reasonable, and tourists as a whole prefer hiring to bringing their own cars, or, alternatively, they take guided tours by bus or taxi. However, in peak tourist periods early booking is advisable. The smaller firms may try to hire out inadequate cars. Insist on a recent model.

To hire a car, you need a valid driving licence, and some companies may ask to see your passport. Most agencies set a minimum age for car hire at 25. Reputable firms accept major credit cards as payment, though some may ask for a cash deposit. The rates on page 105 include tax and third-party insurance.

And, before you actually set off, don't forget you're in a left-hand drive country…

Chauffeur-driven cars. This way of sightseeing is a lot more comfortable than driving yourself on the rather difficult roads—if you can afford it. The charge per hour is high. Some garages impose a minimum rental period of 8 hours. Taxis can also be hired by the hour, half day or day, with prices ranging wildly according to your bargaining skills.

CIGARETTES, CIGARS, TOBACCO*. Some international brands of cigarette are made locally. Maltese makes are less expensive than foreign ones. Major international brands of cigars and tobacco are also on sale.

Cigarettes and tobacco are available in many small shops with no special identification, except for a display which makes it clear they sell tobacco. Some shops may be marked "tobacconist".

CLOTHING. Light and loose cotton clothes are the best daytime items for the hot summer. Women usually prefer fullish skirts—cooler than slacks. Everyone should have a hat or scarf for protection from the sun, and comfortable rope- or rubber-soled shoes or sandals for sightseeing (different styles are available locally, though they're not strictly high fashion).

But heat doesn't mean you can go around half-dressed. The Maltese are on a campaign against unseemly dress in public places (bathing costume, bare midriff).

The strict Maltese Catholic ethic prohibits shorts, miniskirts, low-cut or shoulder-baring dresses while visiting churches. Women may be handed a scarf to cover shoulders.

Although bikinis are now a common sight at beaches, the topless look and nudity are illegal, and you risk a fine or worse if you try.

In the evening, certain luxury hotels and the casino require jacket and tie for men; women may want one or two informal long dresses or skirts or dressy trouser-suit combinations. Take a jersey or a wrap for cooler evenings.

In winter, the climate demands light woollen clothing, jackets, jerseys, possibly a spring coat or a raincoat.

COMMUNICATIONS

Post offices. Postal service is generally quite efficient in Malta. The General Post Office at Auberge d'Italie in Merchants Street, Valletta, keeps the following hours:

Summer (June 16 to Sept. 30), 7.45 a.m. to 6 p.m., Monday–Saturday
Winter, 8 a.m. to 6.30 p.m., Monday–Saturday

Branch post offices are open from 7.45 a.m. to 12.45 p.m., Monday–Saturday all year round.

The main branch post office on Gozo is at 129, Republic (Racecourse) Street, Victoria. Hours are the same as Malta's.

Stamps may also be bought at most hotels, some tobacconists and some shops that sell postcards.

Poste restante (general delivery). If you wish to have your mail sent to you c/o poste restante, you should write ahead of time to warn the post office (address the letter to the Postmaster General, General Post Office, Valletta, Malta).

Telegrams. You can send telegrams from the Telemalta Corporation in South Street, Valletta, from 8 a.m. to 6.30 p.m., Monday–Saturday (except on holidays), and at Luqa airport every day from 7 a.m. to 7 p.m. Alternatively, the Main Telegraph Office (open 24 hours a day) is in St. George's Road, St. Julian's.

No local telegram facilities are provided.

Telex/fax. Your hotel may provide you with telex/fax facilities on request. Public telex/fax facilities are available at South Street, Valletta, and at Luqa airport, from 9 a.m. to 5.30 p.m. Monday–Saturday (except holidays), and at St. George's Main Telegraph Office at the same hours from Monday to Friday (except holidays). Facsimile transmission services are also available at Telemalta main offices in Valletta, Sliema, St. Julian's and Victoria (Gozo).

Telephone. Public telephone boxes, conveniently situated on many streets and squares are painted red. Information in the telephone directory is in Maltese and English. For local calls, you can usually dial direct from your hotel room or by asking the operator for an open line. Some hotels allow non-guests to use their lobby phones.

Overseas calls can be dialled direct to many countries, using the prefix 00-followed by the destination code. For information, dial 194 to get the overseas telephone exchange. Hotels are authorized to add an extra charge for calls placed.

For the directory enquiry service, dial 190.

The country code for Malta when dialling from elsewhere is 356.

COMPLAINTS. If things go wrong, try complaining first to the owner or manager of the establishment. The friendly Maltese invariably try to set things right when you explain your problem. If you are still not satisfied, you can then go to the National Tourist Organization (see TOURIST INFORMATION OFFICES), or call their special number, 605 615, where visitors can lodge complaints. This number is manned during office hours, but at all other times a recording machine registers calls.

If your problem is bad merchandise or car repairs, complain at once to the merchant or car hire firm. If this fails, go to the National Tourist Organization. Complaints made to the police will usually be referred back to the Tourist Organization.

CONVERSION CHARTS. Metric weights and measures are in general use, although there are a few survivals from earlier systems. (Some pubs offer pints of beer, for example.)

Temperature

°C −30 −25 −20 −15 −10 −5 0 5 10 15 20 25 30 35 40 45

°F −20 −10 0 10 20 30 40 50 60 70 80 90 100 110

C Length

COURTESIES. To help you meet the Maltese, there are no "official" organizations, but you really need no such help. The people are proud and dignified yet kind and friendly. If you want to enter into conversation, discuss the beauties of their islands. They may invite complete strangers around for a drink, or to share tea or coffee in a hotel or café. Whenever problems arise, whoever is around will try sincerely to help, whether locating an address, finding a telephone or getting your car repaired. Whether in shops or restaurants, on guided tours, at the beach or a swimming pool, it is easy to meet the Maltese. Young people also mix and meet at the many discotheques.

The islanders have the casual Mediterranean way of looking at things, and "tomorrow" or "later this afternoon" is just as good as "right now" for getting things done. So be insistent, while trying not to hurry them too much. They have a strict Catholic upbringing, and are usually very polite, even sometimes formal, on a person-to-person basis. They treat each other and strangers courteously, and expect the same treatment in return.

Nobody is going to ask you to speak a word of Maltese, but you will get amused and happy smiles if you try out *bonġu* ("good morning") and *bonswa* ("good evening"), *skużi* ("excuse me", pronounced just like in Italian) and *grazzi* ("thank you", almost like Italian). See also LANGUAGE.

CRIME and THEFT. Malta is still relatively crime-free compared with the rest of the world, and tourists are safe almost anywhere. But the incidence of theft is on the increase. It's wise policy to take the usual precautions: deposit your valuables in the hotel safe; if you've rented a flat, don't leave them in a conspicuous place. Lock your car as a matter of principle. Any loss or theft should be reported immediately to the nearest police station, and, if it happened at the hotel, to the hotel management.

The possession, use and distribution of drugs are criminal offences, punishable by fines and/or prison.

CUSTOMS and ENTRY REGULATIONS. See also DRIVING. For a stay of up to three months, a valid passport is sufficient for most visitors.

Here's what you can take into Malta duty free and, when returning home, into your own country:

Into:	Cigarettes		Cigars		Tobacco		Spirits		Wine
Malta	200	or	250 g. of other tobacco products*				1 l.	and	1 l.
Australia	200	or	250 g.	or	250 g.		1 l.	or	1 l.
Canada	200	and	50	and	900 g.		1.1 l.	or	1.1 l.
Eire	200	or	50	or	250 g.		1 l.	and	2 l.
N. Zealand	200	or	50	or	250 g.		1.1 l.	and	4.5 l.
S. Africa	400	and	50	and	250 g.		1 l.	and	2 l.
U.K.	200	or	50	or	250 g.		1 l.	and	2 l.
U.S.A.	200	and	100	and	**		1 l.	or	1 l.

* of which not more than 50 g. in loose tobacco
** a reasonable quantity

Currency restrictions. There's no limit on how much foreign currency a non-resident may bring into Malta (providing it's declared upon ar-

C rival), but you are entitled to import only Lm 50 in local currency. Visitors may export a maximum of Lm 25 in local currency, plus any remaining foreign currency of the sum they brought in and declared to customs upon arrival.

D **DRIVING IN MALTA.** If you're going to go to all the trouble of taking your car to Malta, you'll need

- your national driving licence
- car registration papers
- insurance coverage (the most common formula is the Green Card, an extension to your regular insurance, making it valid abroad)

Though there are practically no standard equipment requirements on Malta or Gozo, it's safe policy to use seat belts, and bring a red warning triangle for use in case of emergencies.

Driving conditions. Take care! is rule number one, especially if you're not used to driving on the left. After a bit of practice, you'll get the hang of it. The rules in general follow those in Great Britain: drive on the left, overtake on the right; in roundabouts (traffic circles), yield right-of-way to cars already in the roundabout circuit.

Speed limits are theoretically 40 kilometres per hour (25 mph) in built-up areas, 64 kph (40 mph) on the larger roads.

The best policy for visitors is to drive defensively, giving large berth to lorries (trucks) and buses, or precedence to aggressive-looking vehicles. Driving in Malta, and especially on Gozo, can be a trial for a newcomer used to order.

In the centre of Valletta, many streets are closed to cars, others are one-way, and the rest are usually clogged.

Road conditions. There are a few stretches of road big enough for four lanes. Both Malta's and Gozo's main central routes, though not always in good repair, are usually wide enough to accommodate two or three vehicles abreast. The roads often have potholes, sometimes repaired by hot tar and an amalgam of stones plus a fine dust topping. Smaller roads are sometimes very poor, and unless you're careful, you may get stuck on a road or country path that narrows down so much that you have to back out. It's best to use the horn when going around what look like sharp corners and hairpin turns, especially in small villages.

Parking. Fines for illegal parking are being enforced. Be absolutely
112 sure not to block anyone, or an exit. There are no parking meters.

If you put your car in a parking lot, give the attendant a small tip when you leave. In the centre of Valletta, the parking problem is acute.

Traffic police. You don't often see them, but they do patrol roads in pairs, whether in cars or on motorcycles. You might see an occasional roadblock for identity checks if the police are looking for criminals.

Fuel and oil. Fuel is available in super (98 octane), unleaded and diesel. Service stations open 7 a.m. to 7 p.m., but close on Sundays, so be sure not to run out of fuel on Saturday night.

Breakdowns. Towing and on-the-spot repairs are made by local garages, and spare parts can usually be found for most current makes of car. If you're renting your car, first call the hire firm who should be able to send help within the hour.

Accidents. In case of an accident, call the police immediately. Dial 191. It is wiser not to move your vehicle until the police arrive, since accident claims are not usually settled unless the police make a report on the spot.

ELECTRIC CURRENT. Electric supply is universally 240-volt, 50-cycle A.C. The three-pronged British plugs and sockets are used. Australian and New Zealand visitors will need an adaptor, Americans a transformer.

EMBASSIES and HIGH COMMISSIONS

Australia	High Commission, Airways House, Gaiety Lane, Sliema; tel. 33 82 01
Canada	Embassy (Italy), Via G. Battista De Rossi, 27, 00161 Rome; tel. 85 53 41
New Zealand	Embassy (Italy), Via Zara, 28, 00198 Rome; tel. 844 86 63
United Kingdom	High Commission, 7, St. Anne Street, Floriana; tel. 23 31 34
U.S.A.	Embassy, Development House, St. Anne Street, Floriana; tel. 62 36 53/62 32 16/62 04 24

E **EMERGENCIES.** In case of accident or other emergencies, phone:

Police	191
Ambulance	196
Fire	199

For traffic accidents, see under DRIVING.

G **GUIDES*.** The National Tourist Organization (see TOURIST INFORMATION OFFICES) can provide you with qualified official guides who must wear a red badge showing they have passed a strict comprehensive test of history and languages. Your hotel can also find a guide for you. For tours guides, tipping is included, but you might give a museum guide a few cents.

H **HAIRDRESSERS*.** Malta's better hair stylists are generally well up on the latest styles and cuts. If you're swimming and in the sun a lot, it's a good idea to ask for a hair conditioner.

Some hairdressers are listed in the *What's On* guide. The bigger hotels also have good hairdressing salons.

Hairdressers are usually tipped about 10 to 15%.

HEALTH and MEDICAL CARE. In this warm and humid climate, as in many similar places, newcomers may contract "tourist's tummy", often due to fatigue, too much sun and change of diet. Food and drink are quite safe, but be sure fresh fruit and vegetables are washed.

The water is generally safe for drinking, but it is often unpalatable. Do not drink water from fountains. Water in hotels and homes comes straight from the "mains", and is therefore safe. Most mineral water is imported. The local brand, slightly bubbly, is *San Michele*.

Don't quaff too much of the local wine—excellent but with potent laxative effects for the unwary in the case of the cheap, common variety. If gastro-intestinal or other problems last more than a day or two, see a doctor.

Beware of the sun, which is very powerful in the summer months. Start with a sun-cream screen or complete-block (total) cream at first and build up a tan gradually in small doses. The occasional salt tablet doesn't do any harm when you're perspiring a lot.

There are plenty of insects in country areas around Malta and particularly on Gozo, especially in the hottest part of summer. But don't worry, there are several sprays available in the shops if they bother you. Small, invisible flies can leave itching bites; for these, use the insect repellent and itch-remedy creams obtainable at the pharmacy. The same goes for mosquitoes. If you should have mosquitoes in the room, buy an inexpensive coil called "moon tiger", which burns all night and keeps them away. Even more effective (more expensive as well) is the electric version of this. Both can be purchased at chemists.

Insurance. Malta has a reciprocal agreement with Great Britain, providing nearly the same free health care the British service offers. But if you come from elsewhere, make sure your health insurance policy covers accident or illness while on holiday—it's simply a wise precaution.

Treatment. You may not get served in the hospital on silver platters as in the times of the knights, but medical equipment and treatment is usually of a reasonable standard. General practitioners are all Maltese and well qualified.

If you need a doctor urgently, your hotel will help you find one; otherwise, the chemist can be of assistance. In an emergency, you can dial 196 on both Malta and Gozo, or:

Malta, St. Luke's Hospital (Gwardamanġa), tel. 62 12 15

Gozo, Craig Hospital (Għajn Qatet Street, Victoria), tel. 55 68 51

Pharmacies, clearly marked "Chemist" or "Pharmacy", are usually open during normal working and shopping hours. Pharmacies open on Sundays are listed in the local weekend newspapers.

HITCH-HIKING. It is permitted, though not common. If you do so, obey the normal common-sense rules. But it's much better to use the cheap and perfectly adequate bus service.

HOTELS and ACCOMMODATION*. See also YOUTH HOSTELS. Malta .offers everything from luxury hotels to simple guesthouses. Around 100 hotels are rated according to comfort and amenities by the Hotels and Catering Establishments Board, which also puts out various brochures listing all details. Hotel categories range from five-star (the most luxurious) to one-star (the simplest); holiday complexes and aparthotels are rated first, second or third class, guest houses as

H first or second class. Don't take these ratings as an exact guide to quality. And for you, a warm welcome at a so-called second class guest house may outweigh the 24-hour room service at a five-star hotel.

It is imperative to book at the hotel of your choice well in advance if you plan to go during the crowded summer season or even early autumn.

Self-catering possibilities. Many people prefer to rent flats (apartments) or villas for their holidays. Prices and amenities vary. The National Tourist Organization brochure will give details of places listed for rent.

Note: Do not rent from somebody you encounter casually; some of these owners practise systematic rip-offs on unsuspecting tourists from abroad.

HOURS. Everything closes up for a few hours around lunchtime. The summer heat can be unbearable; so do as the locals do—relax until the cool of late afternoon.

Hours of opening vary wildly according to what the establishment is, whether government or private, what day of the week, which time of the year. The following is an indication of the general rules. (See also under COMMUNICATIONS and MONEY MATTERS.)

Government offices. Winter (Oct. 1 to June 15): 7.45 a.m. to 12.30 p.m. and 1.15 to 5.15 p.m., Monday to Friday. Summer: 7.30 a.m. to 1.30.m., Monday to Friday.

Offices and Businesses. 8.30 or 9 a.m. to 1 or 1.30 p.m. and 2.30 to 5.30 or 6 p.m. A few operate on Saturday mornings. Most head or managing offices follow Government schedules.

Shopping hours are generally from 9 a.m. to 7 p.m. with a one- to three-hour break for lunch (usually closer to three), Monday to Saturday. Some establishments remain open during lunch, and some stay open to 8 p.m. on Saturdays.

The open-air market at St. John's Square, Valletta, operates until about noon, Monday to Saturday. On Sundays, a much larger morning market attracts crowds to St. John's Ditch just outside Valletta, a stone's throw from the bus terminus.

Museums. Most museums and sites are state-run and therefore have
fairly uniform hours. Winter (Oct. 1 to June 15): 8.15 a.m. to 5 p.m.,

Monday to Saturday, 8.15 a.m. to 4.15 p.m. on Sundays. Summer: 7.45 a.m. to 2 p.m. including Sundays. All museums are closed on public holidays. In Gozo, museums open one hour later and close one hour earlier.

Mdina Cathedral Museum. Winter (Oct. 1 to May 31): 9 a.m. to 1 p.m. and 1.30 p.m. to 4.30 p.m. Till 5 p.m. in summer. Closed on Sundays and holidays.

Manoel Theatre. 10.45 a.m. and 11.30 a.m. tours, Monday to Friday.

National War Museum (in Fort St. Elmo), same timetable as state museums.

St. John's Co-Cathedral. 9 a.m. to 12.30 p.m. and 3 to 5.30 p.m., Monday to Saturday; from 3 to 5 p.m. on Sundays. The museum and oratory open at the same hours on weekdays, but are closed on Sundays.

The Malta Experience, at Mediterranean Conference Centre: shows at 10.30 a.m., noon, 1.30 p.m., 3 p.m., 4 p.m.; Saturday 11 a.m., noon. Closed Sunday.

LANGUAGE. You can get along fine if you speak English, since nearly every Maltese you'll encounter has a good to excellent command of it. Many speak Italian as well, and some speak French. However, the first language here is Maltese—both fascinating and quite incomprehensible to most foreigners. The pronunciation is especially difficult.

Here is a key to some of the trickier consonants:

ċ – like *ch* in *ch*ild
g – like in *g*ood
ġ – like *j* in *j*ob
għ – silent
ħ – silent, except when preceded by għ
h – *h*
j – like *y* in *y*ear; **aj** is pronounced like *igh* in h*igh*; **ej**, like *ay* in s*ay*
q – like a very faint *kh*-sound, without English equivalent; a bit like cockney "ain't i*t*"
x – like *sh* in *sh*op
z – *ts*
ż – *z*

117

A few everyday expressions:

	Maltese	**pronunciation**
good morning	**bonġu**	BON-joo
good evening	**bonswa**	BON-swah
yes	**iva**	EE-vah
no	**le**	leh
please	**jekk jogħġbok**	yehck YOJ-bok
thank you	**grazzi**	GRAHT-see
excuse me	**skużi**	SKOO-zee
Where is…?	**Fejn hu…?**	fayn oo
right	**lemin**	LEH-meen
left	**xellug**	shehl-LOOG
straight ahead	**dritt il-quddiem**	drit il-KHOOD-dee-ehm
How much?	**Kemm?**	kehm

Numbers

0	**Xejn**	shayn
1	**Wieħed**	WEE-hehd
2	**Tnejn**	tnayn
3	**Tlieta**	TLEE-tah
4	**Erbgħa**	EHR-bah
5	**Ħamsa**	HUM-sah
6	**Sitta**	SIT-tah
7	**Sebgħa**	SEH-bah
8	**Tmienja**	TMEE-ehn-yah
9	**Disgħa**	DI-sah
10	**Għaxra**	AHSH-rah

For the most common town and site names, see under PLACE NAMES.

LAUNDRY and DRY-CLEANING. There are ample laundry and dry-cleaning services on both Malta and Gozo, and Malta has some self-service launderettes accessible to tourists during normal business hours. Laundry service takes about three days, as does dry-cleaning. There are express one-day services, however, and top hotels offer both regular and same-day service, but same-day costs a lot more than the regular.

LOST PROPERTY. Check first where you think you lost the object; the Maltese people are, in general, scrupulously honest about other people's property. If you can't find the object, try at the nearest police station.

Lost children. Don't let young children out of your sight in crowded places (like the swarming main streets of Valletta). If a child is really missing, report it immediately to the police.

MALTA FOR CHILDREN. There aren't many special attractions for children on Malta, but they'll be happy all the same, especially on the beaches. The easy, sandy ones are wonderful for all ages, though you should keep an eye on very young children and toddlers, as there is not much in the way of life-guard service. The rocky beaches can be excellent for swimming and snorkelling or sailing for older children.

The *festi,* or religious festivals, are even more fun for children than for adults. They happen all summer long on weekends (the tourist office can give you a list of where and when). There are parades, perhaps little fairs, and on Saturday evenings the fireworks can be spectacular. Good displays to watch (from afar to avoid the crowd) include the St. George festival in Qormi and the St. Nicholas festival in Siġġiewi, both in late June on Malta, and the mid-August festival in Victoria, Gozo.

Children might like the *Imnarja,* or folklore festival, in Buskett Gardens. Also in late June, just after the folklore festival, is a donkey race at nearby Rabat. Other donkey and horse races to watch: in July, the feast of St. George in Victoria, Gozo, and in August, around the feast of St. Mary (Assumption) on both islands. Carnival parades take place on the days preceding Lent. The regatta—boat races to celebrate Our Lady of Victories—is held on the Sunday nearest to September 8 in Valletta's Grand Harbour.

In St. Anton Gardens, Malta, a few animals and birds are on display.

Baby-sitting services are listed in the local papers and in the *What's On* guide.

MAPS. The tourist offices in Valletta and Victoria, Gozo, hand out a very basic map, which might also be available from your hotel. Otherwise, there's a good choice of maps at bookshops, hotel news-stands, etc.

Currency. The Maltese pound (£m) is divided into 100 cents (¢), the cent into 10 mils (m). Within the country, the pound is referred to as *Lira,* plural *Liri* (abbr. *Lm*).

Notes: Lm 2, Lm 5, Lm 10 and Lm 20.

Coins: 2m, 3m and 5m and 1¢, 2¢, 5¢, 10¢, 25¢, 50¢ and Lm 1.

You won't usually be asked to give out mils, but you might get some back as change.

Malta's gold and silver proof and brilliant uncirculated coins for collectors are sold at the Malta Coins Distribution Centre, Central Bank of Malta, Castille Place, Valletta, at the issue price. Coins whose issue is closed can be purchased at a premium through coin dealers. To take more than a few souvenir coins out of Malta, you'll need a permit from the Central Bank of Malta.

For currency restrictions, see under CUSTOMS AND ENTRY REGULATIONS.

Banking hours. In summer, hours are generally from 8 a.m. to noon, Monday to Friday, till 11.30 a.m. on Saturdays; in winter, banks open and close half an hour later. These are branch office hours in most towns and villages in Malta. Certain banks have foreign-exchange desks open in the afternoons from 4 to 7 p.m. (3 to 6 p.m. in winter).

On Saturdays, banks will usually only change foreign cash up to the value of Lm 100 for bona fide tourists. Many hotels give very low rates of exchange for **traveller's cheques,** so it's usually better to go to a bank. You'll need your passport when cashing traveller's cheques.

Credit cards are widely accepted by better shops, hotels and restaurants in the bigger towns. Usually the symbols of the cards recognized for payment are on display. In shops, pay with Maltese currency or credit cards unless they are advertising a special high rate for your foreign currency.

Prices are fairly reasonable when compared with the big continental cities. Food is inexpensive. Handicrafts (weaving, lace, knitting, pottery, glass, etc.) are good buys (see Shopping, p. 88). Prices are usually fixed, so bargaining is no good, but you can try haggling at small shops and street stands. Certain rates are listed on page 105 to give

you an idea of what things cost.

NEWSPAPERS and MAGAZINES. All the British dailies and the *International Herald Tribune* are usually available in the afternoon of the day of publication (the next day on Gozo) at most news-stands. There is one English-language daily published in Malta, *The Times,* and three weeklies, the *Sunday Chronicle* and *The Democrat* (Saturday) and *The Sunday Times.*

The small fortnightly *What's On* guide gives a vast amount of information, everything from restaurants and cinemas to tips for the tourist.

PHOTOGRAPHY. There are many spectacular views to interest the amateur or professional, especially where cliffs of pastel-coloured rock tumble into the dark blue or turquoise sea, or in the small alleyways and around the church squares.

Most well-known film brands are available, but not everywhere. Valletta has several good photography shops. You may have trouble finding 35-mm black and white or especially fast film, but major brands of colour print and transparency (slide) film are easy to find.

You may be able to get fast black-and-white development, but it is rare.

Video tape is readily available. Colour print film is processed on a same-day basis on weekdays.

The airport's X-ray machine does not ruin film, but for safety's sake, put it in a bag to be examined separately by the checkers.

PLACE NAMES. See also LANGUAGE. The Maltese like to hear at least their town names pronounced properly. So here's a list of the main sites mentioned in this book.

Birżebbuġa	beer-zeeb-BOO-jah	Naxxar	NAHS-shahr
Borġ in-Nadur	borj in-nah-DOOR	Qala	KHAH-lah
Buġibba	Boo-JIB-ba	Qawra	KHAW-rah
Ġgantija	J'GAHN-tee-yah	Qormi	KHOHR-mee
Għar Dalam	ahr DAH-lam	Saqqajja	sahkh-KHIGH-yah
Għar Ħassan	ahr hahs-SAHN		
Għar Lapsi	ahr LAHP-see	Siġġiewi	SEEJ-jee-eh-wee
Għarb	ahrb		
Ħaġar Qim	hah-jahr-KHEEM	Tarxien	TAHR-sheen
Marsamxett	mahr-sahm-SHEHTT	Xagħra	SHAH-rah
Marsaxlokk	mahr-sahm-SHLOCK	Xlendi	SHLEHN-dee
Mdina	im-DEE-nah	Żebbuġ	ZEHB-booj
Mġarr	im-JAHRR	Żejtun	ZAY-toon

P **POLICE.** Most towns have a police station, clearly marked. Some stations are not manned around the clock. All police officers, whether gazing at the traffic passing by or helping a tourist find his way, are dressed in casual cotton khaki uniforms in summer, black uniforms in winter, with visored hats.

PUBLIC HOLIDAYS. These are the official civic and religious holidays when banks, offices and shops are closed. Not listed are the numerous *festi* on various weekends in towns all over, though shops usually remain open on Saturdays.

January 1	New Year's Day	*August 15*	Feast of the
February 10	St. Paul's		Assumption
	Shipwreck	*September 8*	Our Lady of
March 19	St. Joseph's Day		Victories
March 31	National Day	*September 21*	Independence Day
May 1	May Day	*December 8*	Immaculate
June 7	Commemoration		Conception
	of June 7, 1919	*December 15*	Republic Day
June 21	St. Peter and	*December 25*	Christmas Day
	St. Paul		
Movable date:		Good Friday	

R **RADIO and TV.** Radio Malta broadcasts on two frequencies. One of them, Radio Malta International, puts on programmes in English and Italian.

On short-wave bands, reception of the BBC World Service is clear. Voice of America's programmes are also easily picked up.

Television Malta transmits about five hours of programmes in Maltese and English each evening, including both British and American features. An English newscast is a daily feature.

RELIGIOUS SERVICES. Malta is almost 100% Catholic. Most services are in Maltese. For non-Maltese Roman Catholics, St. Barbara Church on Republic Street, Valletta, celebrates mass in French, German and English at various times. Several other denominations also have churches in Malta; see the weekend newspaper or *What's On* guide, or check with your high commission, embassy or consulate.

TIME DIFFERENCES. Malta follows Central European Time (GMT + 1), and in summer (March 31 till third Sunday in September) clocks are put one hour ahead (= GMT + 2).

Summer chart:

New York	London	**Valletta**	Johannesburg	Sydney	Auckland
6 a.m.	11 a.m.	**noon**	noon	8 p.m.	10 p.m.

Dial 195 for a time check.

TIPPING. A service charge is sometimes included in restaurant bills, but in any case it is customary to leave a small tip on top of it. A bit of loose change for their services is also appreciated by bellboys, hat-check attendants, etc. The chart below gives some suggestions as to how much to leave.

Porter, per bag	10–20 ¢
Hotel maid, per week	50 ¢
Waiter	5–10%
Lavatory attendant	10 ¢
Taxi driver	10%
Hairdresser/Barber	10–15%

TOILETS. There are few public conveniences and only in the larger towns, and the signs designating which is which ("ladies" or "gentlemen") are very subtle—sometimes you have to ask. If you see an attendant, you may give him or her a few cents. "Keep this place clean" cautions one sign in a Valletta convenience, "legal action will be taken". Cafés and bars usually have facilities you can use.

TOURIST INFORMATION OFFICES. There is an Air Malta information desk at the airport, where they can advise about hotels and give other information.

The office to contact for detailed brochures on hotels, self-catering flats, etc., is the National Tourist Organization, 280 Republic Street, Valletta; tel. 22 44 44.

T There is also a tourist information office at:

1, City Gate Arcade, Valletta; tel. 22 77 47

where the staff give brochures and maps and will help with all problems except changing money, though they will point you in the right direction.

In Gozo, go to the Tourist Information Office at Mġarr harbour (near the ferry landing pier); tel. 55 33 43—or in Palm Street, Victoria; tel. 55 64 54.

Tourist Organizations and information for Malta abroad:

Eire	Honorary Consul for Malta, Traverslea, Glengeary Co., Dublin; tel. (01) 80 10 81
United Kingdom	Malta National Tourist Office, Ste. 300, Mappin House, 4 Winsley Street, London W1N 7AR; tel. (071) 323 05 06.
U.S.A. and Canada	Maltese Consulate, 249 East 35th Street, New York, NY 10016; tel. (212) 725-2345/8
	or:
	Embassy of Malta, 2017 Connecticut Avenue N.W., Washington D.C. 20008; tel. (202) 462-3611/2

TRANSPORT. See also CAR HIRE.

Bus services. Maltese and Gozitan towns are linked up by regular and efficient services, though in summer the buses get rather hot and crowded. You pay your fare to the driver. In Valletta, buses for all parts of the island leave from the Triton Fountain just outside City Gate. Destinations are indicated by numbers on the bus, and you can find out which number goes where by asking at your hotel desk, at the Tourist Office, or a bus driver. Buses are pea-green and grey (Malta) or red and silver (Gozo).

In Victoria, Gozo, the main terminal is on Maingate Street.

Ferries. Apart from a summer helicopter link, the only way to get to Gozo is by boat. Services between Malta and Gozo are frequent, but bad weather may render them unreliable. One passenger/car ferry leaves each morning from Sa Maison Pier in Pietà Creek, Pietà for the main Gozo harbour, Mġarr, a trip of 1 hour 15 minutes. It has ample space, a large, air-conditioned passenger lounge and café-restaurant.

Another passenger/car ferry is smaller and less expensive, but often crowded and uncomfortable in summer. It leaves from Ċirkewwa in north-west Malta for Mġarr several times a day, a 20-minute trip. A more luxurious ferryboat on this stretch is the *Mġarr*. From Ċirkewwa, it's quicker, but it means that if you start from Valletta or the airport, you have to drive to the other end of the island.

For further information call 60 39 65 (Sa Maison), 47 18 84 (Ċirkewwa), 55 61 14 (Mġarr) or 55 60 16 (recorded information).

On Comino, the island's one hotel runs a regular boat service to Marfa (on Malta) and Gozo at least six times a day during the season; call 47 34 64/47 30 51 for further details. Also in summer, fast hydrofoil services operate to Gozo from Sa Maison, Sliema and Buġibba.

Taxis. They are clearly marked "Taxi" and have red number plates. All taxis have meters and drivers will dive you an estimate of the cost of the journey. A small tip (about 10%) is expected, especially in cases where the driver has been helpful in carrying your luggage. Cabs are readily available at the airport, as well as at the main hotel, around tourist centres and at the ferry docks. Hotel receptionists will call for taxis.

Horse-drawn cabs. First introduced in the 1850s, the *karrozzin* or horse-drawn cab has now become simply a leisurely way of visiting Valletta, Mdina and Sliema. For a rate definitely to be negotiated in advance, you can tour round for an hour (or more) the main sights of the towns. Pick up a cab at the Customs House or at Great Siege Square in Valletta; at St. Julian's outside the Malta Hilton; in Sliema, try at the harbour ferryboat terminus on the Promenade; and in Mdina, beside Bastion Square or Mdina Gate.

Water-taxis. Somewhat reminiscent of a gondola, the characteristic *dgħajsa* (pronounced "DIGH-sah") or water-taxi with its gay colours, plies the harbours of Malta's main ports. *Dgħajjes* can be hired (at rates to be negotiated) at the Customs House in Valletta and on the waterfronts at Senglea and Vittoriosa.

YOUTH HOSTELS. There are several youth hostels in Malta and one in Gozo. For information, contact the Valletta Youth Hostels Association:

17, Tal-Borġ Street, Paola; tel. 22 93 61

Index

An asterisk (*) next to a page number indicates a map reference. For index to Practical Information, see inside front cover.

Anchor Bay   27*, 63
Arab(s)   15, 16
Attard   27*, 50, 60
   San Anton Gardens   27*, 50, 60, 92

Ballutta Bay   45*, 49
Balzan   27*, 60
Bastions   29, 30, 44, 54
Blue Grotto   27*, 56–57
Boating   86
Boat tours   48, 83
British Rule   22–26
Buġibba   27*, 60
Buskett   27*, 56

Caravaggio, Michelangelo da   10, 39–40
Carnival   92
Cart tracks   14, 67, 80
Casino   93
Cassar, Gerolamo   21, 29, 32, 34, 35, 37, 40, 54, 56
Catacombs (St. Paul's and St. Agatha's)   27*, 55
Churches (see under town headings)
Climate   104
Comino   8, 71, 71*, 83
Cospicua   33, 45*, 47, 48

Delimara Bay   27*, 58
Dingli   27*, 56
Dingli Cliffs   27*, 56
Dragut (pirate)   19, 20, 58, 76

Ferries   63, 70, 105, 124–125
Festivals and festi   9, 54, 56, 72, 74, 90–92
Fishing   86
Floriana   44, 45*
   Phoenicia Hotel   44
   Porte des Bombes   44
   St. Publius Church   44
Food   94–98, 104
Fort St. Angelo   27*, 33, 47
French   16, 22

Gafà, Lorenzo   38, 53, 54, 74
George Cross   24–25
Għajn Rasul   27*, 60–61
Għajn Tuffieħa Bay   27*, 63
Għar Lapsi   56
Golden Bay   27*, 63
Government   8, 26
Gozo (Għawdex)   8, 70–83, 71*, 92
   Calypso's Cave   71*, 80
   Dwejra   71*, 83
   Fort Chambray   71, 71*
   Fungus Rock   71*, 83
   Ġgantija   10, 13, 71, 71*, 77–79
   Għarb   71*, 80, 82
   Marsalforn   71*, 81–82
   Mġarr harbour   71, 71*
   Nadur   71*, 83
   Qala   71*, 83
   Ramla Bay   71*, 83
   San Blas   71*, 83
   Sannat   71*, 80–81
   Ta'Pinu   71*, 82

Victoria (Rabat)   71–76, 71*, 75*
  Cathedral   74–75, 75*
  Citadel   71*, 72, 74, 76
  It-Tokk   73–74, 75*, 90
  Old Town   74
  St. George's Church   74, 75*
Xagħra   71*, 80
Xewkija   71*, 80
Xlendi   71*, 80, 90
Żebbuġ   71*, 82
Great Siege   19–21, 33, 37, 92

Ħaġar Qim (see prehistoric sites)
Ħamrun   45*, 50

Kalkara Ravine   27*, 62
Knights of St. John   17, 18, 19–22

Lace   79, 88, 90
Language   9, 14, 23, 100–101, 117–118, 121
Laparelli, Francesco   21, 29, 32
Lija   27*, 60

Maitland, Sir Thomas, "King Tom"   23, 33
Malta Experience, The   42
Marfa Ridge   27*, 62, 63
Marsaskala   27*, 58
Marsaxlokk   27*, 57–58
Mdina   50–54, 51*, 88
  Church of the Annunciation   51*, 53
  Casa Inguanez   51, 51*
  Cathedral   51*, 52–53
  Cathedral Museum   51*, 53
  Howard Gardens   51, 51*, 54
  Mdina Gate   51, 51*
  Norman House   51*, 54

Palazzo Santa Sophia   51*, 53–54
  Testaferrata Palace   51, 51*
  Vilhena Palace   51, 51*
  Villegaignon Street   51, 51*
Mellieħa   27*, 62–63
Mistra Bay   61–62
Mosta   27*, 58
  St. Mary's Church   58–60

Napoleon   22, 34, 58
Nightlife   92–93

Paola   13, 27*, 68
Peter's Pool   27*, 58
Phoenician influence   14, 36
"Popeye" village   63
Prehistoric sites   13–14, 36, 63–69
  Borġ in-Nadur   13, 64, 57
  Ġgantija (see Gozo)
  Għar Dalam   27*, 66–67
  Ħaġar Qim   10, 13, 27*, 63, 67–68
  Hal Saflieni Hypogeum   13, 36, 63, 68–69
  Mnajdra   27*, 63–64, 67, 68
  Skorba   67
  Tarxien   27*, 36, 64, 69
Preti, Mattia   10, 37, 39, 53, 74
Pretty Bay   58

Rabat   9, 51*, 54–55
  Roman villa and museum   51*, 54
  St. Augustine's Church   51*, 54
  St. Paul's Church   54
  St. Paul's Grotto   51*, 55
Ramla Bay   63
Religion   8, 9, 122
Roger the Norman   16, 50, 53
Roman(s)   14–15, 50

St. Andrew's *45*, 49, 60*
St. George's Bay *27*, 45*, 49, 60*
St. Julian's Bay *45*, 49*
St. Paul *14–15, 55, 60–61*
St. Paul's Bay *27*, 60–61*
Salina Bay *27*, 60*
San Anton Gardens (see Attard)
Sciortino, Antonio *10, 33, 40, 44*
Scott, Sir Walter *28, 37*
Senglea *33, 45*, 47–48*
Shopping *88–90*
Sliema *45*, 48–49*
Sports *84–87*
Suleiman, Sultan *17, 19*

Ta'Qali *27*, 50, 88*
Temples (see prehistoric sites)

Valletta *28–44, 31*, 48*
  Auberges
    ~ d'Aragon *31*, 43*
    ~ de Castile et Léon *31*, 32*
    ~ d'Italie *31*, 34*
    ~ de Provence *31*, 35*
  Churches
    Carmelite ~ *31*, 43*
    ~ of Santa Barbara *31*, 34–35*
    Gesù ~ *41*
    Our Lady of Victories *31*, 32*
    St. Catherine of Italy *31*, 32*
    St. John's Co-Cathedral *31*, 37–39*
    St. Paul's Anglican ~ *43*
    St. Paul Shipwrecked *31*, 43*
    St. Roque *31*, 43*
    St. Ursula *31*, 43*
  City Gate *30, 31**

Fort St. Elmo *31*, 42*
Gardens
  Hastings ~ *31*, 44*
  Upper Barracca ~ *31*, 32–33*
Grand Master's Palace *31*, 40–41*
Manoel Theatre *31*, 43*
Mediterranean Conference Centre *31*, 41, 42*
Museums
  ~ of Archaeology *31*, 35–37*
  ~ of Fine Arts *31*, 37, 43–44*
National Library *31*, 40*
Parisio Palace *31*, 34*
Republic Street *31*, 34*
Squares
  Freedom ~ *32*
  Great Siege ~ *31*, 40*
  Republic ~ *31*, 40*
  St. John ~ *31*, 37*
Triton Fountain *30, 31**
Valette, Jean Parisot de la *17, 19–21, 28, 46*
Verdala Castle *27*, 56*
Villiers de l'Isle-Adam, Philippe *17, 41*
Vittoriosa *17, 45*, 46*
  Auberge d'Angleterre *46*
  Church of St. Lawrence *46–47*
  Freedom Monument *47*
  St. Joseph's *46*

Xrobb-Il-Għaġin *58*

Żabbar *27*, 58*
Zammit, Sir Themistocles *35, 68, 69*
Żejtun *27*, 58*